# The Complete Encyclopedia of
# Wild Game & Fish Cleaning & Cooking

### by Pat Billmeyer

*Volume 3 — Fish, Fowl, Reptiles & Survival*

Illustrated Survival Techniques, Cleaning, Canning & Cooking

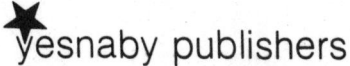
yesnaby publishers

r.d. 8, box 213
danville, pa 17821

Copyright © 1983 by Pat Billmeyer

Published by Yesnaby Publishers, R.D. 8, Box 213, Danville, Pa.   17821

All rights reserved. No part of this book may be reproduced in any manner without written permission from the publisher, except by reviewers who may quote brief passages to be printed in a magazine or newspaper.

Printed and bound in the United States of America.

Library of Congress Catalog Number:   83-50091

International Standard Book Number:   0-9606262-3-9
(Set)
0-9606262-6-3
(Volume)

# Contents

**CHAPTER 1    WILD FOWL**    1-24
Introduction...Drawing...Plucking...Singeing
...Canning...General Information, Cleaning,
Aging, & Cooking of Turkey, Duck, Pigeon &
Dove, Pheasant, Woodcock or Snipe, Quail,
Goose, Grouse & Partridge, and Crow

**CHAPTER 2    FISH**    25-30
Scaling...Skinning...Filleting...Gutting...
Catfish or Bullhead Cleaning...Deboning...
Canning...Drying...Smoking...Building a
Smokehouse...Freezing

**CHAPTER 3    SMALL FRESH WATER FISH**    31-40
Trout...Panfish...Catfish...Perch...Sucker
...Smelt

**CHAPTER 4    MID-SIZED FRESH WATER FISH**    41-44
Pickerel...Bass

**CHAPTER 5    BIG FRESH WATER FISH**    45-53
Muskellunge...Carp...Salmon...Sturgeon...
Roe

**GOD'S CREATURES GREAT & SMALL**    54-64
Crayfish...Eel...Turtle...Frog...Snake...
Snails

**CHAPTER 7    SURVIVAL**    65-82

Survival in a Wooded Area...Building Shelter...Building a Fire...Desert Survival ...Survival Cooking...Survival Tools...Edible Plants...Snakebite

# Wild Fowl

# Chapter 1

## Wild Fowl Cleaning & Cooking

    The greatest arguments concerning the treatment of game must surely be in the game bird category. My husband says his father hung his birds without drawing (gutting) for the entire week he was at hunting camp. Theoretically, the innards dried to a hard ball and when the game got home, it was cleaned, washed and eaten. I maintain that this is not to modern taste. Before regrigeration many palates were accustomed to meat we would consider spoiled today. Also, I am not going to cook or eat any bird without drawing out the entrails. I will, therefore, give directions for birds as I like them. I will also enclose appropriate notes so you may try the old ways if you so desire.

**GAME BIRD DRAWING**
    If you are going to be out in the field all day,

draw the birds when they're shot. Several hours delay aren't too damaging to the taste, but I don't think it improves it any. I know this is in direct contradiction to many gourmets but this book is not directed to them since I assume they know all about their method of treating game. For people who are not accustomed to eating a lot of game birds, draw game as soon as possible.

Put the bird on its back, feet towards you. Cut a circle around the anus, being careful not to cut into the intestine leading to it. Now cut a slit from the anus to the bottom of the breast bone, exposing the entrails. Reach in to the front of the body cavity and gently loosen and pull out the organs. Separate and save the liver and heart.

## GAME BIRD PLUCKING

Right away, I'm in trouble. The dry pluckers, the scalded pluckers and the wax pluckers never give an inch. However:

## DRY PLUCKING

Hold the still warm bird by its feet and pull the feathers toward the head, the opposite of the natural way of their growth. Remove all pin feathers (small feathers which have not yet been removed) and buck shot with tweezers or the tip of a knife. Singe off remaining hairs.

## SCALDED PLUCKING

Bring a large pot of water to a rolling boil. Immediately plunge in the bird holding it by its feet, and swish it gently for about ten to twenty seconds. Remove and immediately pull out the feathers toward the head. Remove pin feathers and buck shot with tweezers or the tip of a knife. Dry the bird and singe off the hairs. This is the method I prefer because I always tear the skin with dry plucking.

## WAX PLUCKING

Remove the coarse guard feathers, leaving all "down" on the fowl. Melt paraffin and cover the bird with hot wax. Allow to cool and pull off. Remove pin feathers and buckshot with knife tip. After plucking, cut off the head and remove the feet at the joints. Slit the skin lengthwise at the back of the neck. Remove the crop and windpipe at the front of the neck. Wash the bird inside and out with clean, running water. Dry and proceed as directed under specific bird.

## SINGEING

Most birds have fine underhair which does not come off during plucking. You must singe this off. Singeing is passing the plucked bird through an open flame. (I use a candle, since I do not have a gas stove.) After singeing, the bird should be thoroughly washed, then proceed with your recipe.

## CANNING RAW

Draw, pluck, singe and wash the birds carefully as directed above. They should be as freshly killed as possible. Aging is not necessary prior to canning. Make sure all shot is carefully removed.

Cut the birds in serving sized pieces. Pack loosely into jars, leaving 1 inch headroom. Add no liquid. Add 1/2 teaspoon of salt to pints, 1 teaspoon of salt to quarts. Wipe rims carefully, put on lids. Pressure-process at 10 pounds (240 F.), pints for 70 minutes, quarts for 80 minutes. Remove jars and complete seals if needed.

FOR CANS: Prepare as directed above. Pack loosely into cans, leaving no headroom. Exhaust to 170 F. in a

# Wild Fowl

slow-boil bath for 50 minutes. Add ½ teaspoon of salt to #2 cans, 3/4 teaspoon salt to #2½ cans. Add no liquid. Wipe rims and seal. Pressure-process at 10 pounds (240 F.) - 55 minutes for #2 cans, 75 minutes for #2½ cans. Remove and cool quickly.

## CANNING PRECOOKED

Draw, pluck, singe and wash the birds carefully as directed above. They should be as freshly killed as possible. Aging is not necessary or desirable for canning. Make sure all shot is carefully removed.

Cut the birds into serving sized pieces. Put them in a large pan and barely cover with boiling water. Cover and simmer for 15 minutes.

Pack the meat loosely into jars and cover with the boiling liquid. Add ½ teaspoon of salt to each pint, 1 teaspoon salt to each quart. Wipe rims and put on lids. Pressure-process at 10 pounds (240 degrees F.) for 65 minutes for pints, 75 minutes for quarts.

FOR CANS: Prepare as directed above. Pack loosely into cans, then add the boiling broth to the top of the can. Add ½ teaspoon salt to #2 cans, 3/4 teaspoon salt to #2½ cans. Wipe rims and seal. Pressure process at 10 pounds (240 F.) for 55 minutes for #2 cans, 75 minutes for #2½ cans. Remove and cool quickly.

# Turkey

A wild turkey can grow to a very large size. A member of our family was in a Mazda station wagon which was attacked by a turkey during mating season. (The turkey's mating season, not my family's.) They said it was so big it was staring into the driver's window.

We have a friend who hunted the wild turkey each

season, without success. Finally, he came into the house bearing his prize, but he didn't look as triumphant as he could be expected to. Later, he admitted he had shot the turkey on his barnyard fence, where it was trying to impress his domesticated hen turkeys.

If there is any moral to these stories, it has to be that during the throes of love, we are all unwise. Let's hope it doesn't turn out to be fatal.

## CLEANING

The turkey is cleaned and plucked as directed at the beginning of the chapter. The wild turkey may be cooked the same way you cook a domestic turkey, except it must be "larded" (salt pork, fat, or bacon must be fixed across the breast and to the drumsticks while cooking, in order to add extra fat). Since they get a great deal more exercise than their domestic kin, they are lean and apt to be stringy.

## AGING

After your turkey has been carefully cleaned and plucked, wrap it loosely in waxed paper and put it in the meat compartment of your refrigerator for 24 to 48 hours.

## ROAST WILD TURKEY
Combine:
1/2 cup or 1 stick butter or margarine
1/3 cup flour

Adding the flour to the butter holds it on the skin during cooking. Rub this mixture into the breast and on the drumsticks, using all of it. Put it into the roasting pan and lay very thin pieces of salt pork or bacon over the breast and the drumsticks, fixing into place with toothpicks, if needed. Put the turkey into a 450 degree

# Wild Fowl

oven UNCOVERED for 1/2 hour, or until well browned. Now, squeeze over it the juice of a lemon, and gently salt and pepper it. Baste it well with the fat from the bottom of the pan, add 1 can undiluted chicken broth or 1 cup water, COVER and roast at 275 degrees for 2½ to 3½ hours, basting every half hour, until very done.

For the last half hour of roasting, add the chopped liver, heart and cleaned gizzard.

## ROAST TURKEY WITH SAUSAGES AND ORANGES

If you aren't sure of the age of your turkey, or even if you are, this is a grand combination.

1 cleaned turkey
1/2 cup flour
1½ teaspoon salt
1 teaspoon pepper
1 pound bulk sausage
2 large oranges
1 teaspoon cinnamon
1/2 cup brown sugar

Clean your turkey carefully as directed at the beginning of the chapter. Cut it into serving sized pieces. Combine in a small bag:

1/2 to 3/4 cup flour (depending on the size of your turkey)
1½ teaspoon salt
1 teaspoon pepper

Shake each piece of turkey in this mixture, pressing through the bag to make sure they are evenly coated. Heat to the sizzling in a fry pan:

1/2 cup butter or margarine

# Chapter One

1/2 cup all purpose shortening

    Brown the turkey pieces on all sides in this sizzling fat.
    Grease a LARGE glass dish or wide-bottomed pan and line the bottom thinly with 1/3 pound sausage. Press into this the browned turkey pieces. Cover the top of the turkey with 2/3 pound sausage. Add 1 cup water, COVER and roast in a 325 to 350 degree oven for 1 hour, then lower the heat to 300 degrees and roast for 1 hour more. Cover the top evenly with the whole sliced oranges, and the brown sugar and cinnamon. Add more water if necessary, COVER and roast for ½ hour more. EXCELLENT!

## Duck

(CANVASBACK, RING NECKED DUCK, REDHEAD (rare), GOLDENEYE OR WHISTLER, MALLARD, TEAL, PINTAIL, WOOD DUCK.)
    Not commonly eaten are: SCALP DUCK, BUFFLEHEAD, OLD SQUAW, SCOTER, HARLEQUIN, BLACK DUCK, GADWALL, RUDDY, BALDPATE, SHOVELER, MERGANSER.

    My husband, Alex Billmeyer, says the woodduck is the most beautiful and the best eating of all ducks. If you disagree, please address your mail to him.

    Legend has it that in the winter, the Delaware Indian painted his canoe white, laid flat in the bottom of it, and floated with the broken ice until he was in the middle of a flock, where he proceeded to get his dinner.

# Wild Fowl

## CLEANING
The duck is drawn and plucked as directed at the beginning of this chapter. The oil sacs at the base of the tail must be carefully removed before cooking.

## AGING
Epicures say the duck must be hung for 24 - 48 hours before cooking. I wrap the cleaned duck loosely in waxed paper and put him in the meat keeper of the refrigerator for 24 - 48 hours.

## HUNGRY MAN DUCK
Some ducks are not usually eaten because they eat fish or water animals which give them a disagreeable flavor. If your duck is one of those, or if you aren't sure exactly what your duck is, this is a good way to go.

Draw and pluck the duck as directed at the beginning of the chapter. Make sure the oil sacs at the base of the tail are removed. Singe and wash well. Ingredients:

1 duck
1 cup undiluted chicken bouillon or 1 cup water
1/4 to 1/2 cup white wine (optional)
1 tablespoon lemon juice, if wine is not used
1/4 pound salt pork or bacon, sliced thin
1¼ teaspoons garlic salt, or plain salt
1 orange or 1 tart apple
1 large onion

Rub the duck inside and out with the salt. Cut the orange or apple and the onion in quarters and put it inside the duck. Lay the bacon over the breast and the legs. Place it in an oiled pot and pour the liquid ingredients around it. COVER and roast in a 350 degree oven for 1 to 1½ hours - until fork tender.  Discard the fruit and onions before serving.

**DUCK WITH SAUERKRAUT**
This is also a great dish if you are unsure about the age of your duck, because the sauerkraut acts as a tenderizer.
Draw and pluck the duck as directed at the beginning of the chapter.  Remove the oil sac at the base of the tail and wash carefully inside and out.

1 duck
2 large cans sauerkraut, drained and washed thoroughly in a sieve, to get rid of the preserving brine.
1 large chopped onion
2 teaspoons salt
4 thin slices bacon
3 cups water

Combine the washed sauerkraut, onion, 1 teaspoon salt and water.  Put it in a deep pot.  Rub the duck inside and out with the other teaspoon of salt and place him on top of the sauerkraut.  Put the bacon over his breast and legs, COVER and roast in a 325 degree oven for 3 hours.  Add more water during cooking if it is needed.  Serve with dumplings and/or mashed potatoes, with melted butter poured over all.

**REMINGTON MALLARDS**
During hunting season, Remington farms in Maryland serve many mouth-watering meals of wild duck cooked like this:

1 cleaned wild duck, with oil sac removed
1 tablespoon sherry or 1 tablespoon lemon juice
½ teaspoon celery salt

# Wild Fowl

½ teaspoon onion salt
½ teaspoon celery seed
¼ teaspoon curry powder
1 teaspoon salt
¼ teaspoon pepper
1 onion, chopped
1 chopped stalk celery
1½ cups water

Sprinkle the duck with the sherry, then with the next six ingredients. Let it stand one hour. Put it in the roasting pan with the water, the onion and the celery. Bake it at 500 degrees until brown, turn it over and bake at 500 degrees until the back is brown. COVER and turn the heat down to 300 degrees. Bake for one more hour. I do not think anyone can improve on this.

## Pigeon & Dove

(TIPPLER, ORIENTAL SHARPSHOOTER, BOHEMIAN OR POUTER, TUMBLER, ROLLER, SQUAB, CARRIER, HOMING, JACOBIN, PASSENGER)
(DOVER, TURTLE DOVE OR MOURNING DOVE.)

The dove is really a smaller breed of pigeon. All American pigeons are edible, although we commonly eat squab which are young pigeons that have been raised for eating. My father-in-law lived when they still slaughtered great flocks of pigeons by catching them in nets. He said the shouts would come from farm neighbor to neighbor - "Pigeons! Pigeons!"

They would run to the barn and get the huge nets which were suspended in the fields about 6 feet above the ground. Underneath they spread corn.

## Chapter One

At that time, he said the pigeons came like black clouds, so that they darkened the sky. When they came down to eat the corn, the nets were dropped. Back then, a large farm owner fed 10 to 20 people all summer, and sometimes all winter. The pigeons were a welcome addition to the cookpot and, since they were so numerous, they were a scourge to the farms.

The old people said that from one year to the next, the pigeons disappeared. One year they came in clouds, the next year there were almost none. Nobody could eat that many in one year. The only answer to their sudden disappearance had to be disease.

### AGING

Neither the pigeon or the dove should be aged. They should be drawn, plucked, singed, washed, and used as soon as possible. If they cannot be used the same day they are taken, they may be wrapped loosely in waxed paper and kept in the meat keeper until the next day.

### BROILED PIGEON OR DOVE

These must be younger birds. Pluck, draw, remove feet and head. Wash out thoroughly, making sure lungs and blood clots are removed. Split them down the back and flatten them with a rolling pin. Pour oil over them, lightly salt with onion salt and pepper and sprinkle them with 1 teaspoon Italian seasoning or dried parsley. Let them marinate at least an hour, turning frequently.

Put them, skin side down, on a flat pan and put in a 375° F. oven for 15 to 20 minutes, depending on their size. Turn them over and slip them under the broiler, about 6 inches from the flame, until browned nicely, brushing with the marinating oil. Serve immediately with baked oranges.

Wild Fowl

**BAKED ORANGES**

This is a marvelous accompaniment for game, particularly game fowl.

Put oranges in a saucepan and cover with water. Bring to a boil and simmer them for one hour. Drain. Cut them in half, put them in a baking dish and pour over them a syrup made from 2 cups sugar, 1 cup orange water and 1 tablespoon lemon juice. Cover and bake in 400° F. oven for 30 minutes. Serve hot or cold.

**ROAST PIGEON OR DOVE**

I loved to eat these as a child, because I got a whole one to myself, and I thought that was quite elegant! Of course, the adults get two or three.

Draw, pluck, singe and wash the birds. For each 4 birds, make the following quantity of sausage stuffing:

1/4 to 1/2 pound sausage
1 cup diced bread
1/4 teaspoon salt
1/4 teaspoon pepper
1/4 teaspoon italian seasoning or mixed herbs

Stuff the cavities with the stuffing and skewer shut. Bring ¼ cup butter to sizzling in a roasting pan and brown the birds on all sides. Then put them breast up in the pan, add 1 cup water or canned chicken bouillon or wine and water, as you prefer. COVER and roast in 350 F. oven for 1 hour, or until fork tender.

# Pheasant

Our section of the country (Central Pennsylvania) was famous for pheasant hunting. We still have them, but they aren't nearly as numerous as they once were.

## TO JUDGE THE AGE

Old pheasants may be known by the length and sharpness of their spurs. In the young ones, their spurs are short and blunt. Also, a young pheasant has a pliable upper beak and a pointed rather than a rounded first wing feather tip.

## AGING

Epicures say the pheasant should be hung for four days to a week, but I wrap the pheasant loosely in waxed paper and put him in the meat keeper of the refrigerator. I have read recipes which instruct you to soak the bird in baking soda water, but DON'T. It tastes awful.

I'll put my favorite recipe first because I'm very proud of it.

## ROAST PHEASANT WITH ORANGE SAUCE

Clean and pluck as directed at the beginning of the chapter. Rub inside and out with a cut lemon, salt and pepper. Lay thin slices of salt pork or bacon over the breast and legs and truss. Roast them in a 350° oven for about 40 to 50 minutes. (Test for doneness at the joint.) Remove to a hot platter and keep warm.

## ORANGE SAUCE
Combine:

Juices from the roasting pan
1 clove garlic, crushed
1 can undiluted chicken broth
1 can orange marmalade
2 tablespoons orange liqueur

# Wild Fowl

2 tablespoons cornstarch mixed to smooth paste with ¼ cup water

Bring to a boil. Simmer gently for 3 minutes. Serve over and with pheasant.

## PHEASANT FRICASSEE
A great casserole dish which can be made ahead and should always be tender, no matter what age your bird.

Draw, pluck, singe and wash the pheasant as directed above. Cut him into serving sized pieces. Dip the pieces into milk, then flour to coat. Bring to a sizzle in a pan, 1/2 cup butter or margarine and brown the pieces on all sides. Arrange the browned pieces evenly in the bottom of the pan and add:

2 sliced carrots
2 sliced stalks of celery
2 large onions, cut into large pieces
2 cups chicken bouillon or water
1/2 teaspoon italian seasoning or mixed herbs
1 teaspoon salt
1/2 teaspoon pepper

COVER and put into a 375 degree oven for ½ hour, then turn down to 325 degrees and roast for 1 hour more, until the bird is fork tender.

Now, make sure you have about 2 cups of broth in the pan.

Combine until perfectly smooth:

2 tablespoons flour
1/4 cup water or sherry
1/2 cup cream or undiluted evaporated milk

Add this to the liquid in the pot, bring to the boil and barely simmer for 5 minutes. Taste and adjust seasoning. Serve with rice or noodles.

# Woodcock or Snipe

Gourmets eat these small birds entrails and all. I don't. Gourmets also hang them for three to four days. I wrap the cleaned bird loosely in waxed paper and put it in the meat keeper of my refrigerator for 24 to 48 hours. Your decision must be your own. I must add that we consider them a delicious delicacy when cooked the following way. Each person has 2 woodcock or snipe.

**ROAST WOODCOCK OR SNIPE**
Draw, pluck, singe and wash the birds. Dry them carefully and mix:

1/4 cup flour
1/4 cup butter

Rub this mixture into the birds and put them in a greased casserole, breast side up, in a 425 degree oven for 5 minutes. Reduce the oven temperature to 325 degrees and roast the birds for 25 minutes, basting them every 10 minutes with more butter. Now, lift each bird and put a slice of buttered bread under him. (Trim off the crusts if you want to be fancy.) Allow it to roast for 5 to 10 minutes more, until the bread is golden brown. Salt and pepper lightly and serve.

**BROILED WOODCOCK OR SNIPE**
Draw, pluck, singe, wash, wrap and age the birds as I have directed above. Cut the birds in half, straight down the breastbone and straight down the spine. Flat-

ten them gently with a rolling pin, then place inside up, on a broiling pan. Cover with thin slices of salt pork or bacon and broil, 6 to 8 inches from the heat, for 5 minutes. Turn them, cover again with thin slices of salt pork or bacon and broil the same distance from the flame for 5 minutes more. Test for doneness and serve.

# Quail

(QUAIL, BOBWHITE, CALIFORNIA QUAIL, MOUNTAIN QUAIL, SCALED QUAIL AND MEARN'S QUAIL.)

**CLEANING**
Draw, pluck, singe and wash bird as directed at the beginning of the chapter.

**AGING**
All cooks agree that the quail needs no aging. Furthermore, it is so delicate that simplicity is the only thing that does it justice.

**FRIED QUAIL WITH ALMONDS**
1 cleaned quail
1/2 cup butter
1/2 cup almonds, skinned
1/2 teaspoon salt
1/4 teaspoon pepper

Split the quail down the back and gently flatten it with a rolling pin. Get the butter gently sizzling in a frying pan and put in the quail, inside down. COVER and fry for 10 minutes. Turn skin side down and fry, UNCOVERED for about 15 minutes. Remove to a heated meat platter. Gently fry the almonds, stirring continuously. Pour browned almonds and butter over the quail and serve.

## OVEN BROILED QUAIL
Split the quail lengthwise, down the spine and the breast. Flatten each half slightly with a rolling pin. Make sure it is very dry, then rub it heavily with butter on both sides. Broil it at low broiler heat (about 8 inches from the broiler) for 10 minutes on each side. Sprinkle with salt and pepper and serve with extra melted butter.

## BARBECUE PIT QUAIL
Marinate the quail for at least 3 hours or overnight in the following:

1/2 cup oil
1/2 cup white wine or 1/4 cup lemon juice
1 teaspoon sugar
1 chopped onion
1 teaspoon Italian seasoning or mixed herbs
1 teaspoon salt
1/2 teaspoon pepper

Just before cooking, press fine breadcrumbs into the quail and broil as far above the charcoal as possible for about 10 minutes on both sides.

## QUAIL CASSEROLE
Clean quail as directed and rub them all over with fresh lemon. Truss them and lay thinly sliced salt pork or bacon over the breast and legs. Line a casserole dish with fresh sausage or chopped ham and press the prepared birds into it. Sprinkle around the birds:

1 dozen tiny white onions

## Wild Fowl

1/2 pound cleaned, whole mushrooms (or more, if you like them)
2 cups fresh or frozen peas
1 teaspoon salt
1½ cups water or chicken bouillon

Cover and bake in a 350 degree oven for 1 hour. If the quail are not brown enough, run the dish under the broiler briefly.

# Goose

(CANADA GOOSE, BLUE GOOSE, SNOW GOOSE, BRANT AND BLACK BRANT)

It is said that the wild goose mates for life, which is more than can be said for most of the human race.

**PLUCKING AND DRAWING THE GOOSE**
Follow the directions at the beginning of this chapter for cleaning game birds.

**TO JUDGE THE AGE OF THE GOOSE**
An old goose will have large wing spurs and red bill. The young have soft undersides on their bills and down on their legs.

**TO AGE THE FLESH OF THE GOOSE**
I have gotten advice which ranges all the way from aging for 5 days to aging for 24 hours. Personally, after it has been properly drawn, plucked, singed and washed, I like to dry it carefully with paper towels, then rub it inside and out with lemon juice (for tenderizing). Let that dry, then rub inside and out with oil. Then wrap it loosely in wax paper and put it in the

meat keeper of the refrigerator for 24 to 48 hours. If this doesn't do it, nothing will. You may substitute the commercial tenderizer for the lemon if you wish.

**ROAST GOOSE WITH SAUSAGE STUFFING**
In a large frying pan, gently crumble:

1 pound bulk sausage
2 large chopped onions

Simmer this gently, until barely done. (You do not want it browned.) Add:
3 cups cubed bread
1 teaspoon salt
1/2 teaspoon pepper
1 teaspoon, dried, mixed herbs (thyme, parsley, etc.)

Make sure the goose is properly drawn, plucked, singed, washed and aged. Stuff him with the sausage stuffing and skewer shut.
Place him in a roasting pan and secure (with toothpicks) thinly sliced salt pork or bacon over his breast and legs. Add 1½ cups water to the roasting pan. COVER the roaster tightly with foil or the roasting pan cover. Roast in a 350 degree oven for two hours, then in a 300 degree oven for one or two hours more (until it is fork tender).

**WILD GOOSE SOUP**
Queen Victoria Soup, which is listed under grouse, is the best fowl soup I have ever tasted and I advise you to try it if you have an old bird or one of indeterminate age and you want to make soup.

**WILD GOOSE BRUNSWICK STEW**
This is a complete meal and very popular in the

# Wild Fowl

south.

Draw, pluck, singe, wash and age as directed above. Cut it into pieces and put it in a pot with:

2 1 pound cans tomatoes
2 large chopped onions
2 chopped garlic cloves
1 1 pound can lima beans
2 cans undiluted chicken bouillon
2 cups water
1 teaspoon Italian seasoning or mixed thyme, oregano, parsley, etc.
1 teaspoon salt

Simmer gently for 2 hours. Stir through and remove all bones and skin. Add 1 1 pound can of corn and 1 cup mashed potatoes or 1 cup bread crumbs. Heat through gently, taste for seasoning and serve.

## Grouse or Partridge

(PRAIRIE CHICKEN, LESSER PRAIRIE CHICKEN, RUFFED GROUSE, DUSKY GROUSE, SOOTY GROUSE, SPRUCE GROUSE, FRANKLIN'S GROUSE, SHARP-TAILED GROUSE, SAGE GROUSE, EUROPEAN OR HUNGARIAN PARTRIDGE, FOOL HEN, SPRUCE PARTRIDGE.)

The ruffed grouse is the Pennsylvania state bird. My husband insists that I point out that the grouse is the most delicious of all game birds. The partridge shot in the United States is really the ruffed grouse so they will be dealt with together.

Chapter One

## TO JUDGE THE AGE
The grouse is a young bird when it has clean claws, soft breastbone tips and no molting ridge on its legs.

## AGING THE MEAT
In times past they were aged up to two weeks, but that is certainly not for me. I wrap the cleaned bird loosely in waxed paper and put it in the meatkeeper for about 48 hours.

## CLEANING THE GROUSE
Draw, pluck, singe and wash as directed at the beginning of this chapter. Make sure all shotgrains are removed.

If you want to fry, oven broil, or barbecue the grouse, please follow the excellent recipes under quail. The only difference in preparation is that the grouse is aged as directed above, and the quail is not.

## GROUSE STROGANOFF
Draw, pluck, singe, wash and age the grouse as directed. Cut it into serving sized pieces and dip it first in milk, then dredge it in a combination of:

1/2 cup flour
1½ teaspoon salt
½ teaspoon pepper

Fry the floured grouse in sizzling butter until it is golden brown on all sides, then add to the pan:

1 chopped onion
1 cup water or canned chicken bouillon, undiluted
1/2 teaspoon Italian seasoning or mixed herbs

COVER and simmer on low heat for 30 to 45 minu-

## Wild Fowl

tes, until it is fork tender. You should have about 1 cup liquid left. Combine until very smooth:

1 tablespoon flour
1/4 cup water

Add this to the simmering liquid, stirring continuously, then allow it to simmer for 3 minutes. Add 1 cup sour cream, stirring continuously. Taste for seasoning and serve.

### QUEEN VICTORIA SOUP

This is a recipe from a 130 year old cookbook. Any fowl may be used, so feel free to substitute any of the wild fowl in this chapter, particularly if you have some doubt as to the age of your bird.

Draw, pluck, singe and wash your fowl. Put it in a pot with:

3 cups water or chicken broth
1 chopped onion
1 bay leaf
1 teaspoon salt
1/4 teaspoon pepper
1 teaspoon dried parsley, or 1/4 cup fresh parsley

COVER and simmer gently for 3/4 to 1 hour, until the flesh is falling off the bone. Remove the fowl from the pot and discard the bones and the skin, then chop the meat finely. Return the meat to the broth along with:

1 cup bread crumbs
2 finely chopped hard boiled egg yolks
1 or 2 cups cream

Heat gently and serve, garnished with fresh parsley. Truly a soup for a queen.

# Crow

**CROW PIE**

I am including this recipe because
1. I found it in a very old cookbook.
2. Everybody should try something new once in awhile.
3. If times get tough, we may all have to eat crow. (You can take that any way you want to.)
4. This must have been the inspiration for "Four and twenty blackbirds, baked in a pie".

**PREPARATION**

Crows must be skinned and stewed in milk and water before being put into the pie dish; they may then be treated as pigeons. Epicures assert that only the breast must be used, but after the crow is drawn and skinned you may lay it on its breast and make an incision on each side of the spine about $\frac{1}{4}$" wide and remove the meat. This is the most bitter part; the whole bird will now be good for eating.

Draw, pluck, singe and wash as directed at the beginning of the chapter, then follow the directions given above in preparation. Discard the milk and water used in the prestewing:

Prepared crows
1/2 pound steak
3 hard-boiled eggs
1/4 cup butter
1 teaspoon salt
1/2 teaspoon pepper

# Wild Fowl

1 round of pie pastry or puff pastry, big enough to cover the casserole

Butter a casserole dish, dice the steak and lay it in the bottom of the dish. Lightly salt with 1/2 teaspoon of the salt. Now lay in the prepared crows, prepared as directed above, either whole or cut in pieces. Sprinkle with the chopped hard boiled eggs and the butter in small chunks. Salt lightly, pepper, and put on the round of pastry. Put into a 350 degree oven for one hour. Serve it, then write to me and tell me how it tastes, because I don't think I'm going to try it.

# Fish Cleaning & Preparation

# Chapter 2

**CLEANING, SCALING, SKINNING, FILLETING, BONING, CANNING, DRYING, SMOKING, AND FREEZING**

Small fish may be scaled or skinned while large fish may be skinned, scaled, or filleted. USE A SHARP KNIFE. Catfish cleaning is a little different and is at the end of the chapter. Small trout need no scaling or skinning, just wash.

**TO SCALE A FISH** (Scrape off the scales)
Place the fish on old newspapers covering a firm surface. Grab the tail with an old towel or cloth and, beginning at the tail, scrape off the scales with a sharp knife, tablespoon or fish scaler.

# Fish

**TO SKIN A FISH**
Place the fish on old newspapers placed on a firm surface. Grab the head with an old towel or cloth. Run a sharp knife down the length of the backbone. Cut the skin around the neck, loosen it and strip it off towards the tail. Since the skin is slippery, grab it with a cloth or pliers or a fish skinner which can usually be bought in a fish store. If cleaning fish is a "sometime thing", a cloth or pliers is sufficient.

**SUPER SIMPLIFIED SKINNING OF THE FISH**
Simply skewer him on the end of a fork and hold him under the hottest water you have running from the faucet for about 20 seconds, then peel him like a banana. (The Indians suspended him over the camp fire for a few seconds, then peeled him.)

**TO FILLET A FISH** (Cut out choice, meaty pieces.)
Place the fish on old newspapers placed on a firm surface. Wrap an old towel or cloth around your hand and grab the head. (This is to safeguard your hand if the knife slips, and to insure a firm hold on your fish.) Place the knife where the tail joins the body, sharp edge towards the head. Holding the knife at 45 degree angle, cut along backbone to neck. Repeat on other side. Cut off head and throw away everything but two fillets. Place fillets skin side down and cut out rib bones. Now you may loosen and pull off skin or scale it. If you leave skin on, it will impart a stronger, fishy taste to the meat, which some people prefer.

**SIMPLIFIED FILLETING**
With a sharp knife, cut lengthwise on each side of the spine. Now, gently strip the flesh loose from the ribcage to the stomach and cut off.

## TO GUT THE FISH
I could use more aesthetic words such as eviscerate, but in this age of truth let us call a gut a gut.

Cut a gash in the stomach of the fish from his gill to his tail. Don't make a small incision, this is not an appendectomy! Using the point of a tablespoon, your knife, or your fingers, remove the guts. Wash out thoroughly with cold water, making sure no clots remain.

## THE HEAD
You may cut off the head or not, whichever suits you. Personally, I always do, but gourmets often prefer the heads of all small fish, except catfish, left on.

## NOTE TO THE FISHERMAN
The fisherman should NEVER carry around dead fish which have not been gutted. If the fish are kept alive on a stringer they need not be gutted in the field, but if they are not kept alive, they should be gutted and washed out, then tossed in an ice chest. When you get them home, wash them thoroughly and proceed.

## CATFISH OR BULLHEAD CLEANING
My favorite. There are walking catfish, blind catfish, armored catfish, climbing catfish, toothless catfish and plain catfish. The bullheads are considered the prize of the catfish family.

Catfish stay alive for a long time after catching; therefore, first stun the fish with a healthy blow on the head with a wooden mallet, rock, etc.

Grasp the fish over the back of the head with your left hand, placing your first and second fingers up against the pectoral fins or "front side fins". Keep your fingers away from the hard gill covers as they HURT.

# Fish

Cut across back of fish directly above the gills, then run the cut down each side of the gills to the beginning of the belly area. With pliers, grab skin at top of back and pull skin toward the tail and pull skin off. Remove head. Slit belly and remove guts. Wash thoroughly in cold water.

## PRESSURE COOKED, DEBONED FISH

EXCELLENT IDEA. This effectively dissolves the bones of any fish. You can catch a batch of sunfish or any very bony fish which are often thrown away, pop them in the pressure cooker, and forget about buying high priced tuna for salads, fish cakes, sandwiches, etc.

Gut and wash fish. Behead if you want. Put them in a pressure cooker with 1/2 inch water and cook for 45 minutes at 15 pounds pressure. When cool, remove skin and any bones which have not dissolved, which won't be much.

## DEBONED PANFISH

Good way to get rid of bones in a small fish and have cups of sweet meat, if you don't have a pressure cooker.

Scale, gut and behead fish. Drop them into a kettle of boiling, salted water and simmer gently for 15 minutes. Remove fish from water and pick flesh from bones.

## CANNING FISH (except salmon and tuna)

If you receive a large influx of fish, use your pressure canner and can them. Not only will you preserve them, the bones will dissolve as in canned salmon and you can lift off the skin, leaving delicious, deboned fish.

Clean fish thoroughly. Fillet large fish. Cut fish or fillets to jar height minus 1 inch. Soak 1 hour in cold water containing 1 cup of salt per gallon. Drain; pack into pint jars (skin side next to glass), and leave 1 inch of headspace. Place jars without lids into canner and cover with 1 inch of hot water containing ½ cup of salt per gallon and boil 15 minutes. Remove, invert over colander, strainer or canner jar rack and drain 5 minutes. Wipe rims, adjust lids and process 100 minutes at 10 pounds in a pressure canner.

## SALMON CANNING

Cut cleaned fish to jar height minus 1 inch and soak 1 hour in cold water containing 1 cup of salt per gallon. Drain 10 minutes and pack into pint jars (skin side next to glass), leaving 1 inch of headspace. Adjust lids and process 100 minutes at 10 pounds in a pressure canner.

AT ALTITUDES OF 2,000 FEET, process at 11 pounds pressure for same amount of time if using dial gauge canner.

## FISH DRYING (SALT CURING)

Behead right behind the gills, leaving the bony structure. Slit lengthwise up the stomach and gut. Slit lengthwise up the spine, cutting the fish into two halves. Remove the spine and ribs. You now have two fillets.

Soak the fillets in salt water (1 cup salt to 1 gallon water) for several hours. Drain.

Using 1 pound of pickling salt for 4 pounds of fish, coat the fish liberally, pressing the salt into all surfaces. Put them on a slatted rack, where they can drain. Weight the top layer to press out the juice. When they have stopped draining, 2 days to 1 week, run a stout string under the bony structure in the neck and suspend them from cross pieces in a shady, dry place until they are thoroughly dry; they're dry when

# Fish

you pinch the fish and it doesn't leave a mark.

## SMOKING FISH

First, follow the directions above for salt curing. Remember, it is really the salt which preserves the fish. The smoking is for taste, to protect the outside and to dry for further curing.

After you have run the string under the bony structure, rinse and scrub off the salt and hang to air dry. Next, hang the fillets in the smoke box and smoke for a least 100 hours keeping it below 70 degrees F. If the smoking is not continuous, the fish must be refrigerated between smoking sessions.

In many parts of Europe, the fish were simply suspended in the fireplace chimney, and since that fire never went out, because all cooking and heating came from there, it was most adequate.

## BUILDING THE SMOKEHOUSE

I have thoroughly covered building smokehouses in my first volume of this series, the "Big Game" section of "The Complete Encyclopedia of Wild Game and Fish Cleaning and Cooking", so I will not repeat it here. Please refer to that section.

## FREEZING FISH

After reading many involved procedures for this, we simply gut them, wash them carefully, wrap them individually in foil and freeze. Small fish (trout, etc.), are successfully frozen in quart freezer boxes in water. The water seems to keep them from freezer burn. However, I do not try to keep fish in the freezer longer than 3 months. They are too delicate, and should be used as quickly as possible.

# Small Fresh Water Fish

# Chapter 3

## Trout

(BROOK TROUT, BROWN TROUT, RAINBOW TROUT, MOUNTAIN TROUT, STEELHEAD AND CUT-THROAT TROUT)

They are the prize of the small fish. Wily, difficult to catch, and a delicate delight to eat. My stepsons swear you must sneak up on a trout, so they crawl to the stream on their hands and knees when they go trout fishing. They must know what they're talking about because they catch more than anyone I know.

Small trout need not be scaled or skinned, just gutted and washed.

**SAUTEED TROUT**
Scale, gut and wash the trout. Behead or not, as you prefer. Salt and pepper lightly. Put $\frac{1}{2}$ to 1 cup flour

# Fish

in a small brown paper bag. Put the trout in the bag, one at a time, and shake until coated. Bring 5 tablespoons of butter or margarine to a gentle sizzle and lay the trout in the pan. COVER and keep them sizzling gently over a slow heat for 15 minutes. Turn and cook for 15 minutes more UNCOVERED.

Put the trout on a hot platter. Add to the drippings 2 tablespoons of butter or margarine and 1 heaping tablespoon frozen lemonade concentrate. Swirl together over heat for 30 seconds. Pour over trout and serve.

## SCOTCH TROUT

Scale, gut and wash trout. Behead or not, as you prefer. Salt lightly and put on plate, cover with Saran Wrap, and refrigerate overnight. Next day, wipe them and salt lightly. Dip in milk, then shake in bag with oatmeal meal. (Dry oatmeal run 5 seconds in blender or a grinder.) Fry in 5 tablespoons gently sizzling butter or bacon drippings for 15 minutes, COVERED. Turn and fry UNCOVERED for 15 minutes more. Serve with lemon wedges and parsley.

## BROILED TROUT

Scale, gut and wash trout. Behead or not, as you prefer. Cut in half lengthwise along backbone. Place skin down on aluminum foil. Pour on melted butter and sprinkle with lemon juice, salt and pepper. Place 7 inches from heat until done, about 10 to 12 minutes. Spoon drippings over fish occasionally during broiling.

## TROUT WITH CRABMEAT STUFFING

Wash and scale trout. Slit lengthwise down back, instead of belly, and remove spine and bones. Remove guts. Wash cavity thoroughly and fill with stuffing. Wrap each fish loosely around middle with parchment paper or strip of aluminum foil to hold in stuffing. Place in oven proof platter or large frying pan. Mix ½ cup chicken bouillon with 1/8 cup sherry. (If your family isn't used to wine in cooking, omit it.) Pour around trout. Bake, UNCOVERED in 375° oven for 25 minutes.

Put trout on warm serving platter and gently unwrap it and place in warm oven. Add ½ can undiluted mushroom soup to drippings and heat gently. Test for seasoning. Pour over trout and serve.

**CRABMEAT STUFFING**
1 can crabmeat or ½ pound fresh crabmeat
2 beaten eggs
½ chopped onion
1 cup bread crumbs
½ cup chopped celery
Salt and pepper to taste

Whip together with fork until thoroughly blended and light.

# Panfish

(BLUEGILL, SUNFISH, GREEN SUNFISH, SHELLCRACKER SUNFISH, WARMOUTH, BREAM, CRAPPIE, ROCKBASS)

These fish are tasty but boney. They should be sautéed until deep golden brown as most of the bones then seem to dissolve. Be careful when small children eat these because the little bones can catch in their throat. Always serve bread or rolls with fish, and if a bone sneaks down the throat, eat bread immediately.

# Fish

## PANFISH SAUTEED IN BUTTER
Scale, gut, behead and wash thoroughly. Salt and pepper lightly. Put 1 cup flour in small bag and toss fish to coat thoroughly. Lay in 5 tablespoons of gently sizzling butter. COVER and cook 15 minutes. Turn and cook UNCOVERED for 15 minutes more.

## DEBONED PANFISH
The following is a great way to get rid of the bones of small fish and still be left with sweet, white flesh. Scale, gut and behead fish. Drop them into a kettle of boiling, salted water and simmer gently for 5 minutes. Remove fish from water and pick flesh from bones.

## SAUTEED BONELESS PANFISH
Prepare fish as directed above. Get 3 tablespoons butter or ham or bacon fat sizzling gently in pan. Add panfish meat and toss until lightly browned. Serve with lemon wedges.

## FISH LOAF
An excellent way to use a large number of small fish. Prepare fish as directed above in deboned panfish.

3 cups cooked fish
3/4 cups fine bread crumbs
6 tablespoons soft butter or margarine
2 eggs, slightly beaten
1 tablespoon parsley
Salt and pepper to taste

Blend all ingredients thoroughly. Put in buttered loaf pan which has been placed in a pan containing 1 inch of hot water. (This will keep the bottom of the fish loaf from becoming brown. If you prefer it brown, omit the pan of hot water.)  Bake at 375° for 1 hour. Serve plain or with one of the following sauces:

TOMATO AND ONION SAUCE
1 can undiluted tomato soup
1 tablespoon onion juice
½ cup cream or undiluted evaporated milk
1 teaspoon parsley
½ teaspoon celery salt

Heat, beat together and pour mixture over loaf.

CHEESE SAUCE
1 can cheddar cheese soup
½ cup cream or undiluted evaporated milk
¼ pound cheese, diced in small pieces
2 tablespoons sherry, if wine flavoring is wanted
Salt and pepper to taste

Beat together cream and soup, add diced cheese and heat over low heat until cheese is half melted. (I like some cheese lumps to remain.) Taste for seasoning and pour over loaf.

# Catfish

My favorite eating fish. Consult special catfish cleaning instructions at beginning of the chapter. They must be skinned. Beware of the hard gill covers on either side of his neck and the fin on top of his head as they STING you if you touch them.

GOLDEN CATFISH WITH BACON
Skin, gut, behead and wash thoroughly in cold water. In a small paper bag put ¼ cup cornmeal and ⅞ cups

# Fish

flour. Gently salt the fish and shake in bag until well coated. Fry out two strips of bacon and lay on paper towel. Add 2 tablespoons butter or margarine to bacon drippings so entire bottom of pan is well covered with fat. Lay in catfish, COVER and sizzle gently for 15 minutes. Turn fish and cook UNCOVERED for 15 minutes more, until golden brown. Serve with bacon crumbled over the top.

This is my favorite spring dinner. I serve it with dandelion in bacon dressing and boiled potatoes covered with melted butter. I am so fond of this combination that I am going to include my dandelion recipe right here.

## DANDELION WITH BOILED DRESSING

Gather dandelion in spring while small and before it gets in flower. An old meat fork is excellent to dig the plant out of the ground. Cut off root and pick out all dead leaves or grass. Wash the dandelion in three separate waters. Put into a pan with 2 cups water and ½ teaspoon salt. Bring to a boil and boil gently for 15 minutes. Drain off water and proceed with sauce.

## DANDELION BOILED DRESSING

Fry out 2 strips of bacon and put bacon on paper towel to drain. Blend until smooth:

1 beaten egg
3/4 cup sugar
1 tablespoon flour
1 teaspoon ground mustard
1/2 teaspoon salt
1/4 cup vinegar
1½ cups hot water

Pour mixture into bacon fat and bring to a boil.

Turn down heat and beat with egg beater while boiling gently for 1 minute. Crumble bacon in dressing.

Combine prepared dandelion, boiled dressing and 1 hardboiled egg, diced finely. Serve hot with catfish and boiled potatoes and melted butter.

## BROILED CATFISH

If you're in a hurry, this is delicious for catfish, bass, perch or trout.

Skin, gut, behead and wash fish. Cut it in half lengthwise along the backbone. Place skin down on aluminum foil. Pour on melted butter and sprinkle on lemon juice, salt and pepper. Place 7 inches from broiler until done, about 10 to 12 minutes. Spoon drippings over fish from time to time during broiling.

## CATFISH BALLS

Debone fish as directed earlier in this section. Combine:

2 cups flaked fish
2 cups mashed potatoes OR 1 cup bread crumbs
1 beaten egg
Salt and pepper to taste

Shape in balls and fry in deep fat at 350°F. until brown.

# Perch

(WHITE PERCH, YELLOW PERCH)

## PERCH FILLETS SUPREME
Simply, the best!

# Fish

1 large egg white, beaten stiff but not dry
1 pound perch fillets
½ cup finely chopped nuts   (Put nutmeats in blender on grate for 10 seconds.)
½ cup flour
¼ cup cracker crumbs
5 tablespoons butter or margarine

Put flour and cracker crumbs in a bag. Wash fillets in cold water and salt and pepper lightly, then shake in flour mixture in bag. Next, dip in egg whites until covered, then dip in chopped nuts. Lay in GENTLY sizzling butter and sauté slowly for 10 minutes, turn and sauté for 10 minutes more. Serve immediately on hot platter, garnished with parsley.

## PERCH FILLETS IN BATTER
Beat together:

1 cup flour
1 teaspoon baking powder
½ teaspoon salt
1 egg
3/4 cup milk

Dip each perch fillet in batter and drop into hot fat heated to 375° F. Fry until golden brown.

# Sucker

(BUFFALO FISH)

We eat them only in the spring when their flesh is firm. They are not as good in warm weather.

Chapter Three

## BAKED SUCKER
.....My mother's recipe, and she's a great cook! Scale, gut and behead fish. Wash thoroughly.

2 cups sliced onions
½ pound thinly sliced bacon
Salt and pepper to taste

Lay fish in greased baking pan. Lightly salt and pepper inside of fish and stuff with 1 cup sliced onions. Lightly salt and pepper top of fish and cover with 1 cup sliced onions. Cover closely with bacon. COVER tightly with foil. Bake 1 hour at 350° F. Serve. This dish is especially delicious in Spring, as mentioned above.

## DEBONED SUCKER
The tiny bones in the sucker can be a problem if you have small children in the house. The following directions render the bones harmless:
Scale, gut and behead fish and wash. Cut into large pieces, removing large bones. Put into pressure cooker and cook 45 minutes at 15 pounds pressure. The bones seem to disappear. You may use the meat for the fish loaf recipe found under "Panfish", or you can toss it in butter or bacon drippings, taste for seasoning and serve.

# Smelt

(CANDLEFISH)

These fish are technically salt water fish that run up coastal streams to spawn. I am including them because they are most often caught in fresh water.

# Fish

Smelt and candlefish are the simplest of all fish to clean. Spread open the outer gills and, with the forefinger, take hold of the inner gills and pull gently. All inner parts are attached to the inner gills and come out with them. Wash out with cold water and wipe dry. They are cooked whole.

## SAUTEED SMELTS OR CANDLEFISH

Salt and pepper fish and put them on a covered tray in the refrigerator for an hour, or overnight. Before cooking, wipe dry, then dip them in cream or evaporated milk and shake them in a small bag containing $\frac{3}{4}$ cup flour and $\frac{1}{4}$ cup corn meal. Melt $\frac{1}{4}$ cup butter to a gentle sizzle and fry UNCOVERED for 10 minutes, turn and fry UNCOVERED for 10 minutes on the other side. Serve with lemon wedges.

## BREADED SMELTS OR CANDLEFISH

Clean smelts as directed above. Salt and pepper and put them on a covered tray in the refrigerator for an hour or overnight. Wipe dry, then dip in cracker crumbs, then in 1 egg beaten with 2 tablespoons milk, then in cracker crumbs again. Melt $\frac{1}{4}$ cup butter or margarine to gentle sizzle and sauté UNCOVERED 10 minutes, turn and sauté UNCOVERED 10 minutes on the other side. Serve with tartar sauce.

# Mid-Sized Fresh Water Fish

# Chapter 4

## Pickerel

(PICKEREL, BULLDOG PICKEREL, MUD PICKEREL, CHAIN PICKEREL, WALLEYED PIKE, WALLEYE, PIKE PERCH AND GRAYLING.)

Pickerel is the name given to the three smaller members of the pike family. They are: the bulldog pickerel, the mud pickerel and the chain pickerel. The chain pickerel is considered the prize of the family.

The cleaning and cooking directions for the fish listed above are interchangeable. They may be poached, boiled, steamed, sautéed, fried or baked. They are the boniest fish of all so I suggest the pressure cooked, deboned fish recipe at the beginning of the fish section. If you don't mind the bone picking, choose any other recipe.

# Fish

## SCALLOPED FISH CASSEROLE
Butter baking dish and put in a thin layer of sliced potatoes. Salt and pepper lightly and put in a layer of thinly sliced onions. Salt and pepper lightly and put in a layer of flaked fish which has been pressure cooker deboned. Salt and pepper lightly and repeat until dish is full, ending with a layer of sliced onions. Sprinkle with bread crumbs and lay sliced bacon over the top. Pour in ½ cup cream or evaporated milk and ½ cup chicken bouillon. Bake one hour, COVERED, then brown bacon under broiler and serve.

## COLD FISH MOLD
This is a great main dish in the summer and great for a buffet.

Prepare fish in pressure cooker as instructed. Melt 3 tablespoons flour and cook for 2 minutes. Stir in 1 cup chicken broth and simmer until thick. Add 1 tablespoon curry powder, 2 cups of cooked rice and 2 cups of flaked fish. Add ½ cup of heavy cream, whipped, or 2 cups of some Dream Whip or Cool Whip. Put mixture in an oiled 1½ quart mold, cover and refrigerate for 6 to 12 hours. Unmold and garnish.

Because of their bones, I do not believe in putting pike, pickerel or grayling in batter or thick coating. If you do not want to pressure cook them, try the following.

## BROILED PIKE, PICKEREL OR GRAYLING
Fillet fish as instructed. Place fillet, skin side down, on oiled broiling tray. Salt and pepper lightly and pour on melted butter. Broil 7 inches from the broiler until done, about 10 to 12 minutes. Serve with lemon wedges.

Chapter Four

# Bass

(LARGEMOUTH BASS, SMALLMOUTH BASS, KENTUCKY BASS, SPOTTED BASS, REDEYE BASS, WICHITA SPOTTED BASS, ALABAMA SPOTTED BASS, SUWANEE BASS, WHITE BASS, YELLOW BASS)

My husband loves fishing for bass so much that I can hardly get him to go fishing for anything else. He is, of course, a member of the Bassmasters, reads the magazine, has the insignia on his boat, and will probably be one in his next life. How in the world I ever forgot the bass in my first book, I'll never know. Probably a classic example of psychological overkill. I must admit, it is superlative eating.

**BASS FILLETS**
With a razor sharp knife, (the only secret to filleting) cut a long incision on either side of the backbone. GENTLY strip the flesh loose from the ribcage until you cut the piece off at the stomach. Take your time and don't waste the good fish.

If you want to skin the fillet, simply skewer it on a fork and hold it under the hottest water from the faucet for about 15 to 20 seconds, then peel it like a banana.

**BASS IN BATTER**
Put in a frying pan and bring to the gentle sizzle:

½ cup vegetable shortening
¼ cup butter
  Combine:
½ cup flour
¼ teaspoon baking powder
½ teaspoon salt

# Fish

1 medium sized egg
Enough ICE WATER to bring the mixture to the consistency of heavy cream

Beat this mixture until it is frothy. The secret of the good batter seems to be in having it as cold as possible, and not too thick.

Dry your fillets and dip them in the batter. Put them in the hot fat and fry them in medium heat (not smoking, but sizzling), for 5 to 8 minutes on each side. Serve immediately with tartar sauce.

## BROILED BASS

Scale, gut and behead the fish, then flatten him with the flat side of a knife. Soak him overnight in the following marinade:

½ cup oil
2 tablespoons lemon juice, or frozen lemonade mix
1 teaspoon garlic salt OR 1 teaspoon salt
1 crushed clove of garlic
1 teaspoon soy sauce

Broil 6 to 8 inches from the fire, watching carefully and brushing with the marinade until done - about 6 minutes on each side.

# Big Fresh Water Fish

# Chapter 5

## Muskie, Pike & Gar

(MUSKELLUNGE, MUSKIE, SALMON PIKE, WHITE PICKEREL, CHAUTAUQUA MUSKELLUNGE, LAKE TROUT, NORTHERN PIKE, GAR, LONGNOSE GAR OR BILLFISH, SHORTNOSE GAR, ALLIGATOR GAR.) --- The Gar is edible, although often not eaten---

These large fish may be poached or boiled, steamed, baked whole or in pieces. However, since they may run from 8 to 60 pounds, the method of cooking will have to be dictated by the success of the fisherman. Few cooks have the facilities to bake a 60 pound muskie whole, although the concept is intriguing.
Because these fish are so large, they are ideal for the fish canning recipe at the end of Chapter 2. Remember, pressure canning melts the bones, leaving you with beautiful meat.

# Fish

Also, if the bones of the pike bother you, as they do many people, use the pressure cooker deboning process in Chapter 2. Why buy high priced canned fish when, with little effort, you can have your own boneless fish?

## PLANKED MUSKELLUNGE
Fillet fish and wash. Place fillets, skin side down, on a plank of hickory, oak or ash. (You can put them on a cookie sheet if you have no plank but it'll lose a little of the romance.) Salt and pepper lightly. Sprinkle ½ cup of melted butter or margarine over the top, then 1 cup of seasoned bread crumbs. Bake at 350° F. for 25 minutes. Brown briefly under the broiler and serve immediately.

## POOR MAN'S LOBSTER
Fillet and wash fish. Place serving sized pieces of skinned fillets on pieces of foil. Lightly salt and pepper. Sprinkle lightly with lemon juice, then cover with thin slices of butter or margarine. Close foil tightly and bake 20 minutes at 375° F. Serve with individual dishes of melted butter to dip it in, just like lobster. SUPER!

## WHOLE BAKED SMALL MUSKIE
Scale, gut and wash. Behead or not, as you prefer. Stuff the fish with the following dressing. Combine:

1 or 2 cups bread crumbs (depending on size of the fish.)
¼ cup chopped onion
¼ cup chopped celery
¼ cup melted butter
2 tablespoons parsley
1/8 teaspoon tarragon

Salt and pepper to taste

Grease the pan. Put a piece of clean muslin, cheesecloth or greased foil on the bottom of the pan, so you can lift it out in one piece when it is done. Cover the top of the fish with thinly sliced bacon. Bake COVERED in a 350° F. oven allowing 15 minutes to the pound. UNCOVER it for the last 15 minutes of cooking. Serve garnished with parsley and lemon wedges.

# Carp

(SCALE CARP, MIRROR CARP AND LEATHER CARP.)

Scale carp and mirror carp have scales and must be scaled, gutted and beheaded or not as desired. Leather carp are almost bare, with only a few scales, and for all practical purposes will need only gutting and beheading.

Personally, I only eat carp taken in the spring as their flesh is firm then and they do not have the muddy taste they are apt to have later in the summer.

**CARP SIMMERED IN BOUILLON**
Melt:

3 tablespoons butter or margarine
Brown in butter:
½ cup chopped carrots
½ cup chopped celery
½ cup chopped onions

Add:

# Fish

½ teaspoon parsley
¼ cup wine or champagne vinegar, or a white wine
1½ cups water
½ cup undiluted chicken bouillon or broth
Salt and pepper to taste

When the bouillon is boiling, lower the Carp which has been placed in cheesecloth or any clean, white cloth. This keeps the fish together and makes him easy to lift in and out. You can dispense of the cloth and just flop the fish in but it will be tough trying to get him out in one piece. When the bouillon starts boiling again, turn the heat down VERY LOW so it just simmers until tender. (About 12 minutes to the pound.) Remove it as soon as done and put it covered on a hot platter in a warm place until it is ready to sauce and serve.

## BROWN BUTTER AND LEMON WEDGE
½ cup butter or margarine
4 tablespoons frozen lemonade mix OR
2 tablespoons lemon juice and 1 tablespoon sugar

Heat butter gently until light brown, then stir in lemonade mix or lemon juice and sugar until it froths. Pour over carp and serve.

## GLAZE FOR COLD CARP
Strain the stock in which the carp was boiled and reduce it (boil hard until it evaporates) to 1½ cups. Add lemon juice, salt and pepper to taste. Soak 1 tablespoon gelatine in ½ cup cold water.

Add to hot stock. Chill it. When it is about to set, pour it over the cold fish and chill thoroughly. Serve it on a platter garnished with watercress, lettuce or parsley, radishes, deviled eggs, and olives.

# Salmon

Since this chapter is devoted to fresh water fish, I will deal here with the landlocked salmon of Northeastern North America, which averages from 4 to 6 pounds.

Salmon may be boiled, or steamed, sautéed or fried, broiled or baked. I think it is the most beautiful fish to serve whole, hot or cold at an elegant buffet.

**POACHED OR BOILED SALMON**
Scale, gut and wash fish. Behead or not, but in this dish the head is traditionally left on.

**COURT BOUILLON**
Melt 2 tablespoons butter or margarine. Sauté in butter, COVERED, for 3 minutes:

½ thinly sliced lemon
½ cup chopped celery
½ cup chopped carrots
1 teaspoon parsley
1/8 teaspoon marjoram or thyme

Add:

2 quarts boiling water
½ cup white wine, if your family is used to wine flavoring

When water is boiling, lower in the fish which has been wrapped loosely in cheesecloth or muslin to make the cooked fish easy to remove from the bouillon. Sim-

# Fish

mer it COVERED at 12 minutes to the pound. You may serve this hot or cold. The recipes for both follow.

## HOT POACHED SALMON
Follow the above rule. Remove to a heated platter. Remove the skin on the top from the head to the tail and spoon a little of the court bouillon over the meat, to keep it moist. Decorate it with parsley and deviled eggs and serve it with the following sauces:

## CREAM BUTTER SAUCE
Strain court bouillon and boil it down to 2 cups. Melt ¼ cup butter. Add ¼ cup flour and cook and stir gently for 2 minutes. Add the court bouillon and cook and beat with egg beater until thickened and bubbling. Add salt and pepper to taste, then stir in 1 finely chopped hard boiled egg and 1 tablespoon butter.

## COLD GLAZED SALMON
Follow the directions for poaching. Allow the fish to cool in the liquid and chill it. Remove the skin on the exposed side from the head to the tail. Strain the court bouillon and boil it down to 2 cups. Soak 1 tablespoon (1 packet) gelatin in 1/8 cup cold water. Add it to the hot liquid. Chill it. When it is about to set, spoon it over the fish. Allow it to set, garnish with slices of hard boiled egg and parsley.

## BAKED SALMON
Scale, gut, wash and behead the fish. Melt into the baking pan ¼ cup butter or margarine. Turn salmon in the butter to coat it and add 1 cup evaporated milk or cream mixed with 1 cup of chicken broth. Lightly salt and pepper fish and lay over top thinly sliced onion and sprinkle with parsley. COVER and cook at 350° F. at 18 minutes to the pound.

## Chapter Five

**VARIATION**
Add 1½ teaspoon curry powder or 1 teaspoon mustard to the cream.

# Sturgeon

This is a salt water fish that migrates to fresh water rivers so I am including it in this chapter. Since it is a member of the shark family it has a rough skin and a series of sharp, protruding spines running along its body. A great advantage in eating this fish is that since it is a cartilage fish, it has no bone.

To clean, beginning near the head, remove the rows of sharp spines on the long strip of external skin. Next, remove fins. When all five rows of spines and fins have been removed, skin the fish.

Next, you must remove the notochord or spine. Cut around the base of the tail, making sure not to cut through the spine. Carefully pop the tail away from the torso with steady, pulling pressure. The spine will remain attached to the tail section. One long, steady pull will remove the spine from the hollow cavity of the fish. The spine must be removed or the fish will be bitter.

Now, cut the meat into 1½ inch boneless steaks for cooking. If there are roe, save them. They are currently going for about $9 a pound.

Sturgeon may be poached, boiled or steamed, whole or in pieces, or they may be broiled or baked.

**BROILED STURGEON WITH LEMON BUTTER**
Whip together:
¼ cup soft butter or margarine
1 tablespoon lemon juice

# Fish

¼ teaspoon salt
½ tablespoon chopped parsley

Place prepared sturgeon steaks, 1½ inch thick, on broiling pan and spread with ½ of the lemon butter. Broil 7 inches from the heat until it is light brown. Turn, spread with the rest of the lemon butter and broil again until brown.

## SAUTEED STURGEON STEAK
Heat 4 tablespoons butter or margarine until it is gently sizzling. Put in prepared fillets and sauté UNCOVERED for 8 minutes. Turn and sauté UNCOVERED 8 minutes more. Remove to a hot platter. Add to the pan drippings 3 tablespoons butter or margarine and 1 heaping tablespoon frozen lemonade mix or 1 tablespoon lemon juice and one tablespoon sugar. Heat and stir until frothy and pour over steaks. Garnish with parsley and serve.

## BAKED, FILLED FILLETS OF STURGEON
Butter muffin tins. Line them with rather thinly sliced fillets, lightly salted, allowing them to overlap. Fill them with the following stuffing. Combine:

2 cups soft bread crumbs
¼ cup chopped onion
½ cup melted butter or margarine
¼ cup chopped celery
¼ teaspoon poultry seasoning
Salt and pepper to taste

Close fillets over top of the stuffing and put a slice of butter or margarine on the top. Place the tins in a pan of hot water and bake in a 375° F. oven for ¾ to 1 hour. Unmold the fillets on a hot platter.

## ROE (Fish eggs)

Cover the roe with boiling water to which ½ thinly sliced lemon and salt to taste have been added. Bring to the simmer, DON'T BOIL, and simmer gently for 15 minutes. Allow to cool, drain and remove membrane. Proceed with the following recipe.

## CREAMED ROE

Preboil the roe as directed above. Mash them.

Melt 3 tablespoons butter or margarine. Sauté 2 tablespoons finely chopped onion until lightly brown. Add the roe with 2 tablespoons flour.

Brown lightly, then stir in ½ cup cream or evaporated milk. Cook and stir until thick and creamy. Remove from the fire and add two beaten egg yolks. Serve over hot buttered toast or in patty shells.

## ROE SAUTEED IN BACON DRIPPINGS

Fry out 4 slices of bacon. Put bacon on paper towel to absorb the grease. Put in roe that have been prepared as directed above and sizzle GENTLY on both sides until brown. If you get the heat too high, the roe will start to explode and you will think you're cooking machine gun bullets. Even though you keep the heat low you may be wise to partially cover the pan to protect yourself and the kitchen floor. When brown, put on a hot platter and crumble bacon over the top.

# God's Creatures Great & Small

# Chapter 6

And now to the more alien life forms; our flesh and blood brothers and sisters who crawl, hop and sometimes slither.

We all hope for the same things-- to have plenty to eat; to stay warm in the winter and cool in the summer; to have our own way in all things and to rule the world.

I cannot help you with the last part but I am doing my best to see that you succeed in the first. Remember, calm courage conquers all!

## Crayfish

(FRESH WATER SHRIMP)

The fisherman must bring these home alive in a

pail.

It is said that crayfish may be kept alive for severpl days by putting them in buckets containing less than half an inch of water and grasses from their habitat. They require a large amount of oxygen so the water must be continually renewed.

When ready to use, fill a pail with fresh, cold water and add ¼ cup salt.

Let the crayfish set in the salted water for 15 minutes. Bring to a boil a large pot of salted water. Drop the crayfish into the boiling water and let them boil three minutes after they have turned red. Remove them from the water and let them cool. Shuck off the shells and tear off the tiny wing in the center of the tail. This brings with it the small black intestine.

**CRAYFISH COCKTAIL**
   Mix:

1 cup mayonnaise
½ cup catsup
1½ tablespoons lemon juice
Tabasco sauce, if desired
Salt and pepper to taste

Arrange cleaned shellfish in glass. Serve with thin wedges of lemon and sauce in the center.

**FRIED CRAYFISH**
Prepared crayfish
½ cup flour
1 teaspoon salt
1 egg
4 tablespoons cream or evaporated milk

Beat together egg and cream. Put flour and salt in

a bag. Dip the crayfish, first in the egg mixture, then shake in the flour bag. Drop in deep fat heated to 350° F. and fry until brown.
   Serve.

CRAYFISH SOUP
25 to 30 crayfish
1 quart stock (canned chicken broth diluted with equal amount of water will suffice)
½ cup butter
6 anchovies (optional but delicious)
½ cup bread crumbs
¼ cup clam juice (optional)
½ teaspoon salt
¼ to ½ teaspoon pepper

   Prepare the crayfish as directed above, but save the shells. Pound the shells in a mortar, with the butter and anchovies. (You can combine under liquefy in the blender.) Add it to the stock and clam juice and simmer gently for ½ hour. Strain it through a fine strainer and put it back in the pot. Add the bread crumbs and the crayfish and bring to a gentle simmer. Serve.

# Eel

**CLEANING THE EEL**
   An eel must be gutted, skinned and beheaded, in that order. Get an old newspaper or cloth and wrap it around the head. The eel is a little slimy when freshly caught and the paper is to enable you to get a good grip on it. Slit it from its neck to its anus, then gut. Now, cut the skin in a ring around the neck. With pliers, loosen the skin and then pull it all the way off.

## Chapter Six

Cut off the head and wash thoroughly.

A very old cookbook I have says "There is no fish so tenacious of life as this. After it is skinned and cut in pieces, the parts will continue to move for a considerable time, and no fish will live so long out of water.

The lamprey eel was the cause of the death of Henry I, of England, who ate so much of them, that it brought on an attack of indigestion, which carried him off."

You are forewarned that the eel muscles may wiggle while frying or cooking. This is a little eerie but nothing to be worried about.

### SAUTEED EEL

Clean the eel as directed and cut him into 3 inch pieces. Remove the bones. Beat together ¼ cup of salad oil and 4 tablespoons of lemon juice and allow the eel to soak in this for 1 hour, turning frequently. Bring 4 tablespoons butter or margarine to a gentle sizzle and put in the pieces which have been lightly salted and peppered. Sizzle gently, COVERED for 15 minutes, turn and sizzle gently UNCOVERED for 15 minutes more. My mother, who is the sensitive type, says she puts the cover on rather quickly after putting the eel in the frying pan as the moving eel upsets her. As you know your own sensitivities, you may proceed at your own discretion.

### BAKED EEL

Clean the eel as directed above. Remove the backbone. Combine:

1 beaten egg
2 tablespoons lemon juice or frozen lemonade mix

Soak the eel in this for 1 hour, turning frequently.

Put the coated eel in a buttered casserole dish and salt and pepper it. Combine:

½ cup bread crumbs
¼ teaspoon garlic salt
¼ teaspoon pepper

Sprinkle this over the top of the eel. COVER. Bake in a 250 degree F. oven for ¾ hour. Remove the cover and bake ¼ hour more. Serve with tartar sauce.

**EEL STEW**
Clean eel as directed above and cut into 2 inch lengths. Melt in a saucepan 3 tablespoons butter or margarine. Add 2 tablespoons flour and stir gently for 2 minutes. Stir in 1 cup chicken bouillon, undiluted, and beat and cook for 3 minutes or until thickened and simmering. Add 1 can whole onions, 1 can tiny whole carrots and 1 small can of mushrooms, including the broth in the cans. Lay the eel pieces on top of the vegetables. Sprinkle with 1 teaspoon of Italian seasoning, or 1 teaspoon mixed dried herbs. Salt and pepper lightly, bring to the boiling point and simmer gently, COVERED, for 30 minutes. Correct the seasoning and let stand for another 30 minutes. Bring to the boiling point and serve with homemade croutons.

# Turtle

If desired, you may keep the live turtle in a large drum of water for several days, feeding it cornmeal. This "purges" the turtle and gives it a sweet taste.

It takes a rather hardy person to clean a turtle. If you are faint-hearted, pass this book to your favorite "coping" type person. Having forewarned you, let us

press on.
 First, beware of the head. A turtle can bite a lot faster and harder than you would believe. Poke a large, LONG stick at the turtle until he bites fast. Pull his head and neck out and cut off his head with an axe. Now that you have accomplished that, you can do anything. Hang up the turtle by the hind legs to bleed for at least an hour.
 Second, you must procure a pan or a small tub that is a little larger than the turtle. Fill it over half full with water and bring to a good, rolling boil. Place the turtle in the water and cook him for twenty minutes after the water starts boiling hard.
 Remove the turtle from the water and let him cool. Place him on his back and, with a sharp, stiff bladed knife, probe for a soft spot between the two shells. Cut off the belly shell. Remove and skin the legs, tail and neck meat and throw the rest of the mess away. If there are eggs (small, round yellow balls like marbles), save them.

**TURTLE SOUP**
 Bring to a boil:

1 quart water
2 cups beef broth or bouillon, undiluted
2 cups tomatoes
1 teaspoon salt
2 bay leaves
1 teaspoon Italian seasoning (mixed herbs)
$\frac{1}{4}$ teaspoon celery salt

 Add the prepared meat of one turtle and the eggs, if you have them, and simmer GENTLY for one hour. Remove meat and cut into small dice. Replace meat and let sit for several hours, if possible, to meld flavors. Add one cup of mashed potatoes or 2 medium sized potatoes, finely diced and two carrots, thinly sliced. Simmer gently for 45 minutes. Just before serving add ½ cup cream or evaporated milk. Add sherry to taste and salt and pepper if it needs it.

### SAUTEED TURTLE WITH CREAM GRAVY
Bring to a boil:

1 quart of water
½ teaspoon salt
1 bay leaf
½ teaspoon Italian seasoning or mixed, dried herbs
¼ teaspoon pepper

Put cleaned turtle meat in the water and simmer GENTLY, COVERED for one hour. Let meat cool in the broth. Drain well and shake in a paper bag containing 1 cup flour, 1 teaspoon salt and ½ teaspoon pepper. Put 4 tablespoons butter or margarine in frying pan, bring to gentle sizzle, add turtle meat, turning and frying until golden brown, about twenty minutes. If desired, make cream gravy with skillet drippings.

### CREAM GRAVY
To pan drippings, add 1½ tablespoons flour and cook GENTLY until smooth. Add 1½ cups COOL turtle stock. Adjust seasoning with salt, pepper and monosodium glutamate. One-half teaspoon paprika adds a lovely color to gravy if you have it on hand.

### BROILED TURTLE STEAKS
Slice turtle steaks 1½ inches thick. Broil them 7 inches from the flame until they are brown and tender, pouring melted butter over them several times during broiling. Put on a hot platter, pour the broiling pan jui-

ces over them and serve with wedges of lemon.

# Frog

**CLEANING**
　　Make sure the frog is dead. If necessary, whack him on the head with a heavy stick. If you are going to use only the back legs, cut the skin lightly around the midsection. Grab the skin on the back with a small pair of pliers and pull the skin off like taking off your socks. Cut the leg off at the upper joint. If you use all four legs cut the frog lightly around the neck. Grab the skin with a small pair of pliers and pull down until the frog is entirely skinned. Cut off the legs at the upper joint. Wash the legs thoroughly with cold water.

**SAUTEED FROGS LEGS**
　　Soak the frogs legs in milk for 1 hour, turning frequently. Remove them from the milk and salt and pepper them lightly, then coat them with flour. Bring to a gentle sizzle 5 tablespoons butter or margarine and sauté the legs until they are golden brown, UNCOVERED. Serve with hot garlic bread.

**FROGS LEGS IN SHERRY AND MUSHROOM SAUCE**
　　Clean 6 pairs of frog legs as directed above. Bring to a gentle sizzle 4 tablespoons butter or margarine. Add and sauté until light brown on both sides: 1 cup of cleaned mushrooms, sliced or whole. Remove the mushrooms to a hot platter and add 2 tablespoons more butter or margarine to the drippings. Lightly salt and pepper the frogs legs and coat them with flour and sizzle them gently in the butter until they are browned on all sides. Put them on the hot platter and stir into the pan drippings 2 tablespoons of flour. Stir in 1½ cups of chic-

ken broth and simmer and stir until smooth. Add 1 tablespoon of sherry. (More or less to suit your taste.) Serve with hot buttered rice.

# Snake

**SNAKE**

I am not going to pretend that I have cleaned or cooked a snake. However, our game protector, Mr. Richard Donahue, does, and says they are considered a delicacy in much of the world. The directions for cleaning are from him and the directions for cooking are from my good neighbor who says they are delicious.

Cut off the head. Slit down the entire belly to the anal vent. At the windpipe, grab the esophagus and pull the entrails out. Work the skin loose on both sides of the slit and peel off. Wash thoroughly with clean water.

**COOKING**

Cut the meat into 4 inch pieces and drop into boiling, salted water. Boil until it is fork tender but not falling apart. (20 minutes to ½ hour.)

Fry out 4 slices of bacon. Drop the snake pieces in a bag containing ½ cup of corn meal, ½ cup of flour, 1 teaspoon of salt and ½ teaspoon of pepper. Shake the meat to coat it and brown on all sides in the bacon drippings. Crumble the bacon over the top of the meat and serve.

# Snails

**PRE-TREATING**

If you are gathering your own snails, the only advice I could find is, put the snails in a cool and damp place for a month. The snails may have fed on a poisonous plant or substance, and if you starve them for a month, they will be rid of it. I would think it would be more sensible to put them in a deep pot with fresh lettuce leaves in it. They could eat the good food and grow fat, all the while discharging any poison. A month of that should render them safe and tasty.

## CLEANING
Wash the snails thoroughly in cold, clear water. Drop them in a pot of boiling, salted water and cover. When the water resumes boiling, boil 5 to 6 minutes. Drain and let cool. Remove the snails from the shells with a cocktail fork or a nut pick.

## SNAILS IN GARLIC BUTTER
Put ¼ cup butter in pan and set it over medium heat. Add 1 clove crushed garlic and stir gently until lightly browned. Add cleaned snails and swirl until heated through. Taste for seasoning and serve.

## SNAILS IN WINE SAUCE
Put ¼ cup butter in pan and set it over medium heat. Add 1 clove crushed garlic, 1 tablespoon parsley, ¼ teaspoon pepper. Simmer briefly until the garlic is lightly browned. Add ½ cup of dry red wine. Simmer for 5 minutes then turn off heat and let it set for one hour so that the flavors may meld. Bring it to a boil and add one teaspoon of flour which has been mixed with 2 tablespoons of water. Add 2 to 3 dozen cleaned snails and cook gently for five minutes. Taste for seasoning and serve.

## BROILED SNAILS (For 30 to 50 snails)
Combine:

## God's Creatures Great & Small

½ cup (1 stick) butter
2 garlic cloves, peeled and crushed with ¼ teaspoon salt
1 teaspoon parsley

    Clean and precook the snails as instructed above. Put a little of the garlic butter in each shell with each snail and put any leftover butter over all. Put 2 tablespoons white wine or chicken bouillon into a baking dish, arrange the snails in the dish and sprinkle with bread crumbs. Run under the broiler until the crumbs are golden brown and serve.

# Survival

# Chapter 7

The best advice I can give you is --- GET LOST --- for fun, that is. Learn all you can about the plants, wildlife and terrain of the area you will be hunting and fishing in. When you've learned all you can about survival techniques, tell someone where you'll be and camp out for a few days, while your car, with a full gas tank, is right there. Don't cheat! If you can't live off the land for 24 hours, you shouldn't be out there in the first place.

## Survival in a Wooded Area

I hope that no one goes into an uninhabited area without a good knife and several dozen matches in a waterproof container. If you have those two tools and keep your head, you can survive a long while in any

## Survival

kind of weather.

First, if you lose your bearings, put your gun down carefully and climb a tree. Get a good look around. If you see smoke, line it up with trees or other landmarks and set out for it, blazing a trail as you go so you can always get back to where you were, and your friends can follow you.

If you see a stream, you are saved, for you can follow it in the direction in which it is flowing until you come to civilization.

If it is approaching dusk, however, DON'T SET OUT FOR ANYWHERE! You will need any light you have to get comfortable for the night.

If you have a gun, fire it three times in succession, and repeat about every half hour. If you do not have much ammunition, however, don't use it all up in this manner. You will need it to answer if you hear someone signaling you, and you will need it to shoot food. Use your head!

## Building Shelter

You must get out of the wind! Wet your finger and hold it up and you can find out which direction the wind is coming from. You will build your shelter with its back to the wind. If you were equipped for a permanent camp site you would stay out of trees, but in an emergency they provide great shelter, so find a thick grove, particularly pine with low growing branches.

## Chapter Seven

If you are near a stream, make your shelter well above the high water mark in case of a flash flood. If there is a cliff nearby, you are in luck. Try to build your lean to against the cliff with your campfire against it, so the heat is reflected from it.

If the snow is deep enough, dig a hole in a snowdrift big enough for you and your equipment, with your back to the wind.

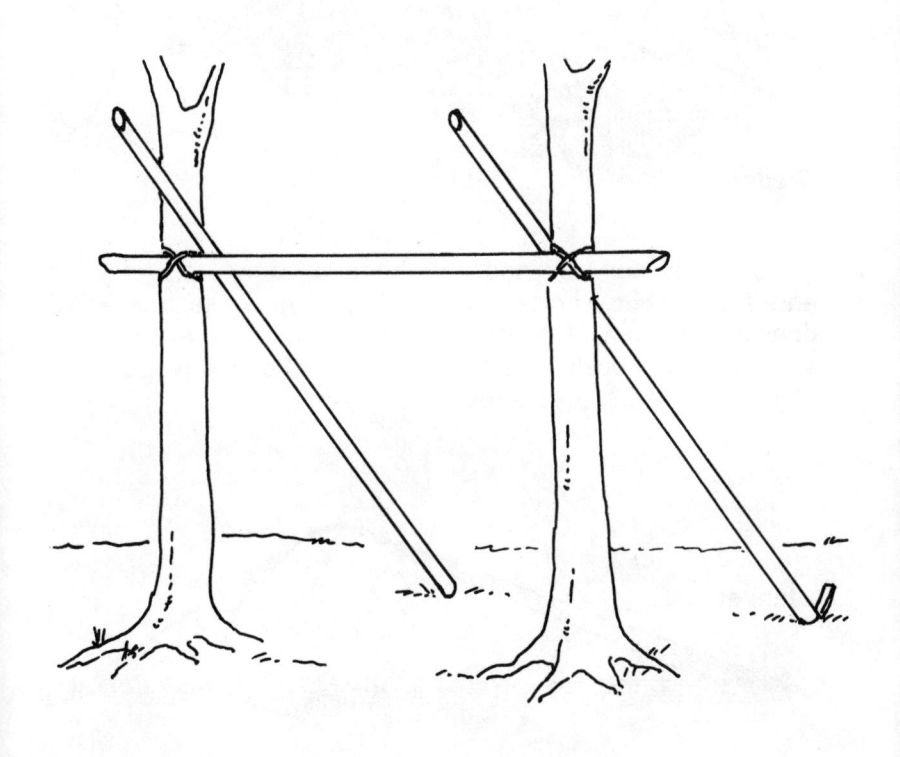

"Lean to"

## Survival

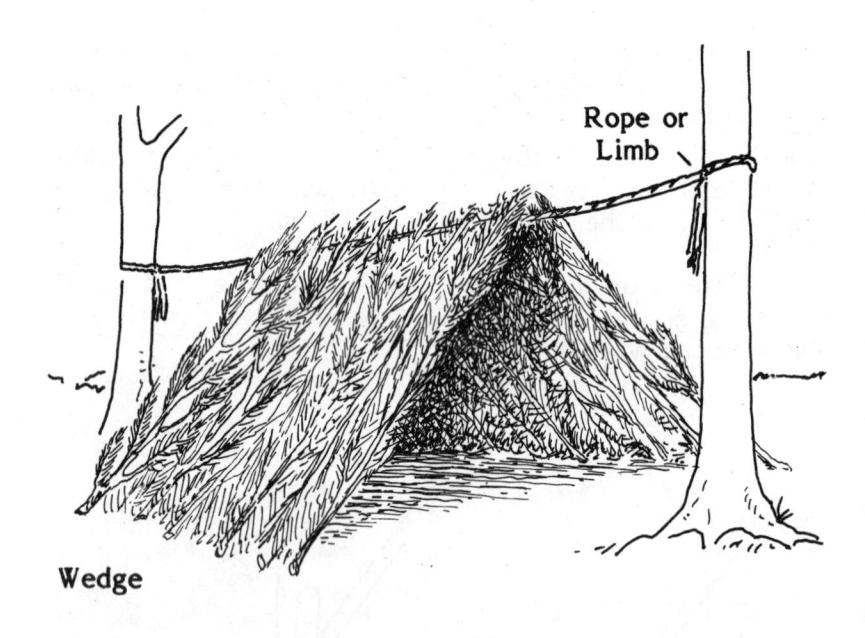

**Wedge** (Rope or Limb)

If it is summer and you have a canoe, tip it over and build your shelter out of it. Tip it so the wind doesn't come in and the rain runs off, and reinforce it with pine or bush limbs. Build far above any possible flash flood - 20 feet above a stream.

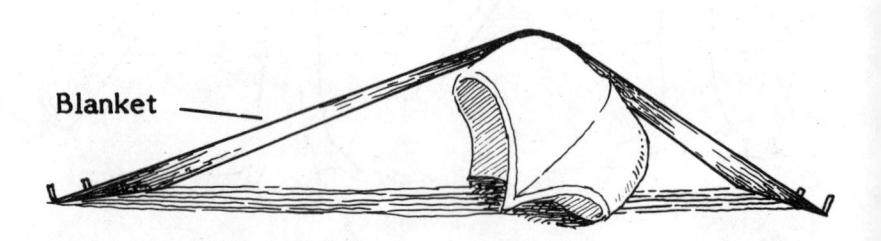

**Canoe Shelter** (Blanket)

Chapter Seven

To sum up building your shelter - take a good look at your assets in the terrain before you make your decision as to the type of shelter to construct. Do as good a job as possible under the circumstances. Wedge the limbs in carefully, make it strong so it won't come down over your head in the middle of the night.

Finally, line your lean to with fine branches or bushes and grass, so you don't get your back wet while you sleep.

## Building a Fire

Gather three kinds of fuel. First, the driest, most flammable such as birds, mouse or squirrel nests or wood shavings. Also, fine twigs and bark, anything that will catch fire easily. Secondly, bigger twigs and pieces of bark, and third, larger pieces to use after your fire is burning soundly. While you're at it, sharpen a sturdy stick to use to hold your meat over the fire. You may have to get your fire lighted on a piece of bark pulled well into your shelter if the wind is blowing fiercely. Don't waste matches! Assemble all your firewood in careful piles in your shelter, ascertain wind direction and shield your match carefully with your hand and body.

Once you have a good fire going, there are several ways of cooking meat. One way is wrapping your food in wet leaves, encasing it in mud and dropping it in the hot coals. Or if you're hungry and not fancy, simply cut it in strips and sear the meat directly on the hot coals. You can skewer it on a stick and rotate it over the fire until it is done to suit you. Save the bones! They can be used with edible plants and water for a

Survival

soup. If you may be out there for a few days, it might be worthwhile building a simple spit.

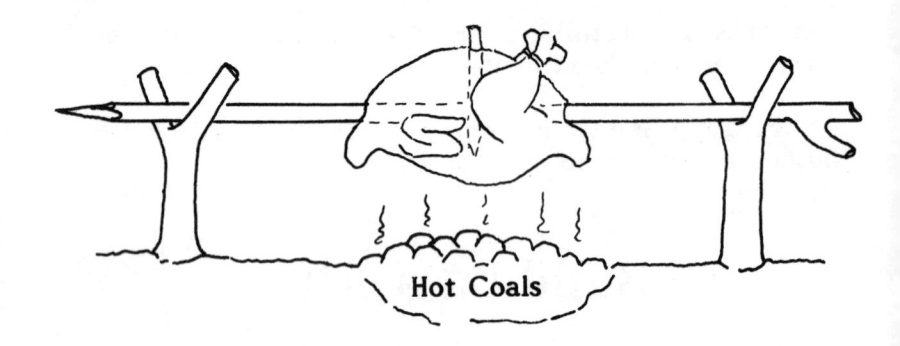

Roasting Spit

# Desert Survival

Ahead of time, let someone know the approximate area you will be in and when you will be back. Give them a panic button time - when to call the sheriff's office for rescue.

Try to get a map of the area, including any place where there is sometimes water.

It helps to have a shovel, a long-handled crow bar and a high-rise jack in case you get stuck, which often happens.

## Chapter Seven

The ground temperature is much hotter than the air, so wear heavy cotton socks and thick-soled boots. Long-sleeved cotton shirts and a hat are a must. They protect from thorns and dehydration. A sheet of plastic can make a "still"; see further on.

You must have a knife and matches, and it will be much easier for you if you have a slingshot, flashlight and first aid kit.

ALWAYS CARRY EXTRA WATER. A gallon a day per person is a rule of thumb; carry enough for 2 or 3 more days than you figure you'll be out there. Having to ration water can lead to dehydration and heat stroke.

When the water supply is getting low, stay in the shade and eyeball the immediate area for action as soon as the evening approaches. In the hills and mountains there are usually potholes of water trapped in the arroyos. Watch where the birds head in the early morning and evening.

The fruit of most cacti is edible and yields a certain amount of water. Folklore has it that cacti marked with spots are not edible. The prickly pear, sahuaro, organpipe and barrel cactus yield some moisture and food value, although the barrel cactus is often too bitter to be of use. The night blooming cereus, which looks like a dry stick, has a moisture laden, nutritious root. If you are going into the desert, it would pay you to get a small book on cacti and study it. The beans from the mesquite and palo verde trees as well as the pads of the prickly pear cactus are also edible.

## Survival

A desert still may be constructed by digging a hole in the ground several feet deep and three or four feet around. Put a container in the center of the hole and lay the plastic over the whole thing. Secure it around the edges with stones, and make it airtight with sand and stones. Put a rock on the plastic sheet directly over the container. The rays of the sun draw the moisture from the soil and condense it on the plastic where it runs into the container. This can create a quart or more of water a day.

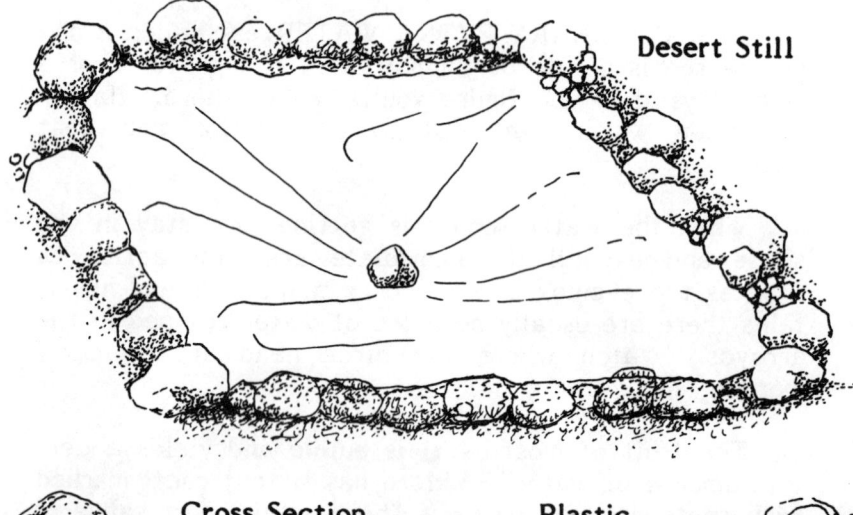

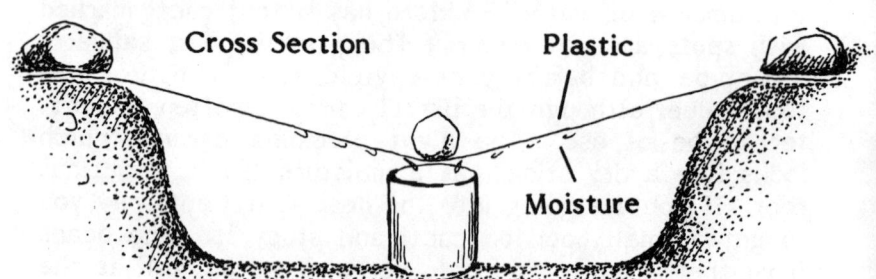

Desert Still

Cross Section  Plastic

Moisture

Can to catch drops of water

## Chapter Seven

# Survival Cooking

For the purposes of this survival section we are assuming that you are lost without salt and pepper, cookpot, or time to spend gathering herbs or seasonings for good cooking. I have already discussed primitive forms of cooking, so I will proceed with the easiest cleaning techniques, as well as glands, etc., which must be removed to make the food edible.

**ARMADILLO OR TEXAS PORKER**
Lay the armadillo on its back and slit the shell lengthwise along its underside. Do not cut through the stomach muscle. Starting at either side, skin the carcass away from the sides of the the shell. After skinning, slit from anus to neck and gut.

**BEAVER**
To eat the beaver tail, simply hold it over hot coals on your skewer. The skin comes off as it roasts and you continue to cook until it is done. The beaver is an exceedingly clean animal and the easiest way to clean it is simply to slit its fur all around the middle and pull both ways. Slit from anus to neck and gut. Cut the animal into smaller pieces and roast.

**WOODCHUCK OR GROUNDHOG**
These are very plentiful in many sections of the country but they have a very tough hide. Cut the skin entirely around the middle, being careful not to cut into the glands in the small of the back. Grab the top part of the skin in one hand and the bottom in the other and pull the skin off like a glove. Remove the glands or kernels from under the front legs and in the

## Survival

small of the back with the tip of the knife, taking care not to pierce them.

### PORCUPINE
The porcupine is protected in many parts of the country because he is so slow and stupid that a person weakened by exposure can easily bag him. They taste like lamb and are easily "dequilled" by singeing them off over the fire. Do this first, then clean in the conventional way by slitting the animal from anus to neck and gutting him. Scrape the skin clean of any fur or quills which may remain and proceed to cook.

### RABBIT OR HARE
For survival purposes we will not bother about the differences between the rabbit and the hare. He is easily skinned and cleaned, but be careful if you have any cuts on the hands as they sometimes have tularemia or rabbit fever which is communicable to humans. Cut the skin around the middle, grab in both hands and pull both ways. Slit from the anus to the neck and gut.

### HOARY MARMOT OR WHISTLER OF THE ROCKIES
He is a cousin of the woodchuck and fine to eat. Cut the skin entirely around the middle, grab with both hands and pull both ways. Cut off around the feet. Slit from the anus to the neck and gut. Remove the glands or kernels from under the front legs and the small of the back.

### PRAIRIE DOG
The tiny Indian brave learned to hunt on the prairie dog, so if you're in the area you should be able to bag one. It, too, has tiny glands in under the front legs and in the small of the back which must be removed. Skin by cutting entirely around the middle,

grab with both hands and pull both ways. Slit from anus to neck and gut.

## MUSKRAT OR MARSH RABBIT

A clean living and delicious animal as long as you remember to remove the glands or kernels in under the front legs and in the small of the back. Cut the skin entirely around the middle, taking care not to pierce the glands, grab the fur in both hands and pull off. Slit from anus to the neck and gut. With the tip of the knife remove the glands, cutting well wide of the glands. Cook and eat.

## OPOSSUM OR POSSUM

The possum is a survivor, one of our oldest orders of animals. He, too, must have the glands removed in under the forelegs and in the small of the back. Cut the skin entirely around the middle, taking care not to pierce the glands in the small of the back. Grab the fur in both hands and pull in opposite directions until the fur is off down to the feet. Cut off the feet, slit the animal from the anus to the neck and remove the guts. Wash out if possible: if not, singe carefully in the fire.

## COON OR RACCOON

This animal has proved time and again that it is smarter than I am, which obviously isn't too hard. Every time I try to grow sweet corn he beats me to the harvest, so I've given it up. He has glands or kernels under the front legs and in the fleshy part of the hind legs, as well as in the small of the back. It is essential that you remove these unbroken. If you were in less desperate straits, you would want to remove the skin in one piece because the hide brings a high price, but the easiest way, if you are hungry and not too strong, is to slit the skin around the center, grab with

# Survival

both hands and pull both ways. Remove the glands, slit from anus to neck, gut and cook.

## SQUIRREL
This animal is plentiful in many places but he is fast. If you're lucky enough to get one he is easy to clean. Cut his skin clear around the mid-section and pull both ways. Slit him from the anus to the neck and gut. Wash and singe if possible, then cook.

## MICE
A tiny morsel but clean and good if you are in an emergency. Skin in the usual way by cutting the fur entirely around the middle, then pull both ways. Slit from the anus to the neck and gut. Singe any leftover fur over the coals, roast and eat.

## SKUNK
The scent glands on both sides of the anus must be removed unbroken, so cut around them, giving them plenty of room. Proceed with cleaning in the usual manner, cutting the skin around the middle and pulling off with both hands. Slit from the anus to the neck, gut, singe the carcass and wash if possible, and proceed to roast the meat.

## PACK RAT
This animal has a musky odor when it is alive, but the meat is said to be sweet and tasty when cooked. Slit him from the anus to the neck and gut. Cut the skin entirely around the middle, grasp in both hands and pull off the skin. Singe, wash and roast.

## SNAKE
In our culture, eating a snake sounds awful, but they are a delicacy in many parts of the world. They

provide clean, boneless meat that is said to be excellent. Simply cut off the head. Slit down the entire belly to the anal vent. At the windpipe, grab the esophagus and pull the entrails out. Work the skin loose on both sides of the slit and peel off. Cut and roast.

## TURTLE

Beware of his head. A turtle can bite faster and harder than you would believe. Poke a stick at his head until he bites fast, then pull his head and neck out and cut off his head. Next, place him on his back and probe for a soft spot between the two shells. Cut off the belly shell. Remove and skin the legs, tail and neck meat and throw the rest of the mess away. If you have time to scrape out the upper shell and have water, you can make a stew by putting the meat back in the cleaned shell with water to cook. More likely you will just section the edible meat and roast.

## FROGS

For survival eating, the easiest way is to simply cut off the head, slit from the neck to the anus and remove the guts. Simply lay the whole frog on the coals, watching carefully and turning until the meat is done. You can simply cut out the meat as you would a fish.

## LIZARD

The same thing is true about the lizard as the frog. For survival eating, cut off the head, slit his belly from the neck to the anus and gut. Lay the lizard on the coals, turning often, until it is done. If you are in the desert, gut and skin the lizard and cut the meat into thin strips and lay it in the sun. The sun will cook it in a very short time.

Survival

## ALLIGATOR
Frankly, if you can catch and kill an alligator I don't think you need any help from me. However, in case this does happen, all my sources tell me to simply cut off the tail and roast it on the coals, since this is where the famous "alligator steak" comes from.

## CRAYFISH
If you are near a stream there are often crayfish lurking under rocks in the shallow water. They are easily cleaned. Simply tear off the tail and the guts come with it. They are so small that your biggest problem will be losing them in the fire.

## FRESH WATER MUSSELS
In streams mussels are often found lying in the open. In ponds or lakes they often burrow at least partially in the mud. Simply wash them, lay them on the coals until they open, and eat.

# Survival Tools

## SIMPLE SPEAR
For small animals, fish or frogs. Cut a stick about six feet long and skin the bark from one end for about a foot. Split it down the center 6 to 8 inches, and put a wedge in it. Whittle in barbs, and bind it tightly around the wedge with a piece of cloth torn from your shirttail, or any place you can get it.

## FISH HOOK
If you have any pins on your person, a bent pin is a real find. Fish hooks can be whittled from a flat, rectangular piece of wood.

## Chapter Seven

**BOLA**

Tear strips of cloth (eight or ten if possible) about 1 1/2 foot by 1 inch. In the end of each piece tie a pebble. Tie them all together at the other end. You will probably find many refinements to this very basic pattern, but it is a simple, effective weapon. Whirl it over your head at your quarry, bird or animal.

**BOOMERANG**

Get a large, flat piece of wood and whittle it into a slightly bent or curved shape.

**STONE AXE**

This is simply a matter of finding a stone the right size and shape, then chipping away the end to make it sharper. It is a harder matter to set it in a wooden handle when you have nothing to fasten it in securely, so since this is survival only you can probably serve your needs with the axe head.

**COMPASS WATCH**

Hold your watch flat and point the hour hand toward the sun. South will be halfway between the hour hand and twelve on the dial.

**DIRECTION BY THE STARS**

The two stars forming the edge of the Big Dipper always point to the North Star.

**DIRECTION BY PLANTS**

The flowers of the compass goldenrod always point north. The leaves of the rosin-weed and prairie-dock always point north and south.

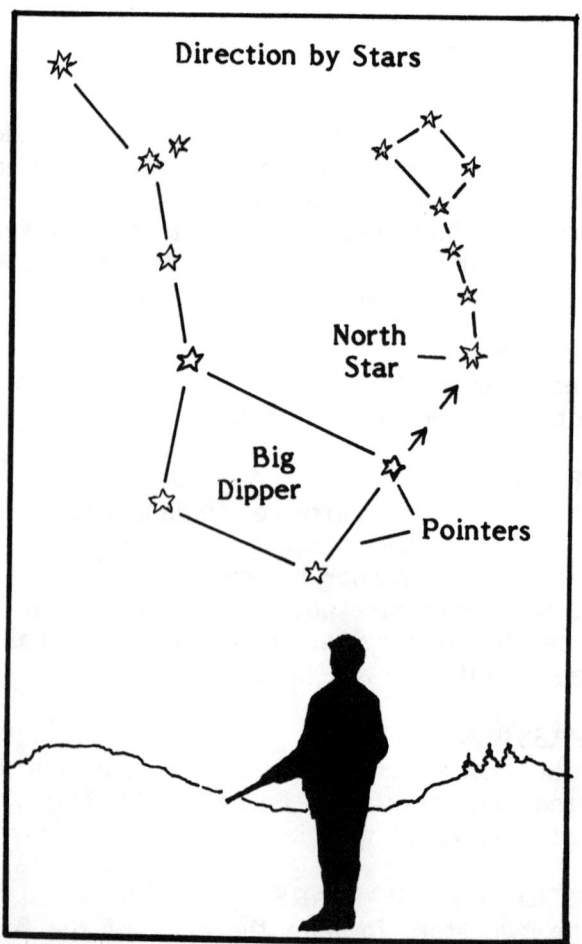

Survival

**Direction by Stars**

Big Dipper · North Star · Pointers

## EDIBLE PLANTS

If you are serious about survival, you must get a book describing the plants in your area and study it carefully. Try to gather a specimen of each of the edible plants in your area and know which parts can be eaten. Learn, also, of the poisonous ones so you'll make no mistake.

Some of the more common edibles are the dande-

## Chapter Seven

lion, chickory, shoots of milkweed, young seed pods of milkweed, leaves of mustard, shoots of burdock, young clover, young grapevine shoots and grapes, etc.

Poisonous ones to avoid are poison ivy, poison oak and sumac, Jimson weed, Pokeweed, White snakeroot, death camas and buttercups.

The Geisinger Medical Center Poison Center in Danville, Pa. says don't eat mushrooms! We could not ascertain any hard and fast rule about eating mushrooms - not even about which mushrooms to avoid. The first problem is that some mushrooms are poisonous in their button stage but not when they are mature. Also, many poisonous ones are nearly the same as their non--poisonous neighbors. Unless you're an expert, don't take a chance.

### SIMPLE TORCH
Split the top of a heavy stick and insert pieces of dry bark.

### BARK UTENSILS
Soak the bark. Cut it in rectangular shapes. For a spoon simply gather it at one end and tie it. For a dinner bowl, simply gather it at both ends and tie it. Infinite variations are possible.

### SNAKE BITE
Poisonous snakes usually make one or two punctures while non-poisonous snakes make a row of punctures. Profuse bleeding from the puncture is another sign of poisonous snake bite. If there is any doubt, treat as follows:

1. Put a not too tight tourniquet between the

## Survival

puncture and the heart.
2. Make short crosscuts over the punctures about 1/4 inch deep.
3. Suck out the venom.
4. If swelling develops, make shallow incisions over swelling and suck out fluid.
5. Do not give the victim alcohol and get to a doctor as soon as possible.

# Index

Alabama Spotted Bass - See Bass
Alligator                              78
Alligator Gar - see Muskellunge
Armadillo                              73
Axe                                    79
Baked Oranges                          12
Baldpate - see Duck
Bark Utensils                          81
Bass                                   25-27, 43, 44
    Broiled                      44
    Fillets                      43
    In Batter                    43, 44
Beaver                                 73
Beheading fish                         27
Billfish - see Muskellunge
Black Brant - see Goose
Black Duck - see Duck
Bluegill - see Panfish
Blue Goose - see Goose
Bobwhite - see Quail
Bohemian - see Pigeon
Boiled dressing                        36, 37
Bola                                   79
Boomerang                              79
Brant - see Goose

# Index

Bream - see Panfish
Brook Trout - see Trout
Brown Butter & Lemon Sauce    48
Brown Trout - see Trout
Buffalo Fish - see Sucker
Bufflehead - see Duck
Bulldog Pickerel - see Pickerel
California Quail - see Quail
Canada Goose - see Goose
Candlefish - see Smelt
Canning Fish    28, 29
Canning Fowl    3, 4
    Precooked    4
    Raw    3, 4
Canvasback - see Duck
Carp    25-27, 47-49
    Brown Butter & Lemon Sauce    48
    Cleaning    25-27, 47
    Glazed    48, 49
    Simmered in Bouillon    47, 48
Carrier - see Pigeon
Catfish    25-28, 35-37
    Broiled    37
    Catfish Balls    37
    Cleaning    25-28
    Golden with Bacon    35, 36
    With Dandelion & Boiled Dressing    36, 37
Chain Pickerel - see Pickerel
Chautauqua Muskellunge - see Muskellunge
Cheese Sauce    35
Compass Watch    79
Cooking, Survival    69
Coon    75
Court Bouillon    49, 50
Crabmeat Stuffing    32, 22
Crappie - see Panfish

# Index

| | |
|---|---|
| Crayfish | 54-56,78 |
|     Cleaning | 54,55 |
|     Cocktail | 55 |
|     Fried | 55,56 |
|     Soup | 56 |
| Crow | 23,24 |
|     Casserole | 23,24 |
|     Preparation | 23, 24 |
| Cut-throat Trout - see Trout | |
| Dandelion with Boiled Dressing | 36, 37 |
| Deboning Fish | 28 |
|     Deboning with Pressure Cooker | 28 |
| Desert Still | 72 |
| Desert Survival | 70 |
| Direction by Plants | 79 |
| Direction by Stars | 79, 80 |
| Dove - see Pigeon | |
| Drying Fish | 29, 30 |
| Duck | 7-10 |
|     Aging | 8 |
|     Cleaning | 8 |
|     Hungry Man Duck | 8, 9 |
|     Remington Mallards | 9, 10 |
|     With Sauerkraut | 9 |
| Dusky Grouse - see Grouse | |
| Edible Plants | 80 |
| Eel | 56-58 |
|     Baked | 57, 58 |
|     Cleaning | 56, 57 |
|     Sauteéed | 57 |
|     Stew | 58 |
| European Partridge - see Grouse | |
| Filleting | 26 |
|     Simplified skinning of fillet | 26 |
| Fire Building | 69 |
| Fish Hook | 78 |

# Index

Fool Hen - see Grouse
Freezing Fish — 30
Fresh Water Shrimp - see Crayfish
Frog — 61,62,77
    Cleaning — 61
    In Sherry & Mushroom Sauce — 61, 62
    Sautéed Legs — 61
Gadwall - see Duck
Game Birds — 1-24
    Canning — 3, 4
    Drawing — 1
    Plucking — 2, 3
    Singeing — 3
Gar - see Muskellunge
Glaze — 48, 49
Goldeneye - see Duck
Goose — 18-20,1,2
    Age - to judge — 18
    Aging — 18,19
    Cleaning — 1, 2
    Plucking — 2, 3
    Roast — 19
    Soup — 19
    Stew — 19, 20
Grayling - see Pickerel
Green Sunfish - see Panfish
Groundhog — 73
Grouse — 20-23
    Age - to judge — 21
    Aging — 21
    Cleaning — 1,2, 21
    Soup - Queen Victoria's — 22, 23
    Stroganoff — 21, 22
Gutting Fish — 27
Hare — 74
Harlequin - see Duck

# Index

| | |
|---|---|
| Hoary Marmot | 74 |
| Homing - see Pigeon | |
| Hungarian Partridge - see Grouse | |
| Jacobin - see Pigeon | |
| Kentucky Bass - see Bass | |
| Lake Trout - see Muskellunge | |
| Largemouth Bass - see Bass | |
| Leather Carp - see Carp | |
| Lemon Butter Sauce | 48 |
| Lesser priarie chicken - see Grouse | |
| Lizard | 77 |
| Longnose Gar - see Muskellunge | |
| Mallard - see Duck | |
| Marsh Rabbit | 75 |
| Mearn's Quail - see Quail | |
| Merganser - see Duck | |
| Mice | 76 |
| Mirror Carp - see Carp | |
| Mountain Quail - see Quail | |
| Mountain Survival | 65 |
| Mountain Trout - see Trout | |
| Mourning Dove - see Pigeon | |
| Mud Pickerel - see Pickerel | |
| Muskellunge | 25-28, 45-47 |
|     Cooking | 25-27 |
|     Planked | 46 |
|     Poor Man's Lobster | 46 |
|     Whole Baked | 46, 47 |
| Muskie - see Muskellunge | |
| Muskrat | 75 |
| Mushrooms | 81 |
| Mussels | 78 |
| Northern Pike - see Muskellunge | |
| Old Squaw - see Duck | |
| Opossum | 75 |
| Orange Sauce | 13, 14 |

# Index

| | |
|---|---|
| Oriental Sharpshooter - see Pigeon | |
| Pack Rat | 76 |
| Panfish | 25-27,33-35 |
|     Cleaning | 25-27 |
|     Deboned | 34 |
|     Fish Loaf | 34,35 |
|     Sautéed | 34 |
|     Sautéed Boneless | 34 |
| Partridge - see Grouse | |
| Passenger - see Pigeon | |
| Perch | 25-27,37-38 |
|     Cleaning | 25-27 |
|     Fillets in Batter | 38 |
|     Fillets Supreme | 37, 38 |
| Pheasant | 12-15 |
|     Age - to judge | 13 |
|     Fricassee | 14, 15 |
|     Roast | 13, 14 |
| Pickerel | 25-27,41,42 |
|     Broiled | 42 |
|     Cleaning | 25-27,41 |
|     Pickerel Mold | 42 |
|     Scalloped | 42 |
| Pigeon | 10-12 |
|     Aging | 11 |
|     Broiled | 11 |
|     Roast | 12 |
| Pike - see Muskellunge | |
| Pike Perch - see Pickerel | |
| Pintail - see Duck | |
| Plucking | 2, 3 |
|     Dry | 2 |
|     Scalded | 2, 3 |
|     Wax | 3 |
| Pressure Cooking Deboning | 28 |
| Poisonous Mushrooms | 81 |

# Index

| | |
|---|---|
| Poisonous Plants | 81 |
| Porcupine | 74 |
| Possum | 75 |
| Pouter - see Pigeon | |
| Prairie Chicken - see Grouse | |
| Prairie Dog | 74 |
| Quail | 16-18 |
|     Aging | 16 |
|     Casserole | 17, 18 |
|     Cleaning | 16 |
|     Fried with Almonds | 16, 17 |
|     Oven Broiled | 17 |
|     Pit Barbecue | 17 |
| Queen Victoria's Soup | 22, 23 |
| Rabbit | 74 |
| Raccoon | 75 |
| Rainbow Trout - see Trout | |
| Redeye Bass - see Bass | |
| Redhead - see Duck | |
| Ringnecked duck - see Duck | |
| Rockbass - see Panfish | |
| Roe | 53 |
|     Cleaning | 53 |
|     Creamed | 53 |
|     Sautéed in Bacon | 53 |
| Roller - see Pigeon | |
| Ruddy - see Duck | |
| Ruffed Grouse - see Grouse | |
| Sage Grouse - see Grouse | |
| Salmon | 25-27, 29, 49-51 |
|     Baked | 50, 51 |
|     Canning | 29 |
|     Cleaning | 25-27 |
|     Cold Glazed | 50 |
|     Court Bouillon | 49, 50 |

# Index

|  |  |
|---|---|
| Cream Butter Sauce | 50 |
| Hot Poached | 50 |
| Salmon Pike - see Muskellunge | |
| Salt Curing | 29, 30 |
| Scale Carp - see Carp | |
| Scaled Quail - see Quail | |
| Scaling Fish | 25 |
| Scalp Duck - see Duck | |
| Scoter - see Duck | |
| Sharp-tailed Grouse - see Grouse | |
| Shellcracker Sunfish - see Panfish | |
| Shelters | 67, 68, 69 |
| Shortnose Gar - see Muskellunge | |
| Shoveler - see Duck | |
| Shrimp - see Crayfish | |
| Skinning Fish | 26 |
| Skunk | 76 |
| Smallmouth Bass - see Bass | |
| Smelt | 25-27, 39, 40 |
| Breaded | 40 |
| Cleaning | 25-27 |
| Sautéed | 40 |
| Smoking | 30 |
| Snails | 62-64 |
| Broiled | 63, 64 |
| Cleaning | 63 |
| In Garlic Butter | 63 |
| In Wine Sauce | 63 |
| Snake | 62, 76 |
| Snake Bite | 81 |
| Snipe - see Woodcock | |
| Snow Goose - see Goose | |
| Sooty Grouse - see Grouse | |
| Spear | 78 |
| Spit | 70 |
| Spotted Bass - see Bass | |

# Index

Spruce Grouse - see Grouse
Spruce Partridge - see Grouse
Squab - see Pigeon
Squirrel — 76
Steelhead - see Trout
Still, Desert — 72
Stone Axe — 79
Sturgeon — 51, 52
    Baked, Filled Fillets — 52
    Broiled — 51
    Cleaning — 51
    Sautéed Steak — 52
Sucker — 25-27, 38, 39
    Baked — 39
    Cleaning — 25-27
    Deboned — 39
Sunfish - see Panfish
Survival — 65
Suwanee Bass - see Bass
Teal - see Duck
Texas Porker — 73
Tippler - see Pigeon
Tomato & Onion Sauce — 35
Torch — 81
Trout — 25-27, 31-33
    Broiled — 32
    Cleaning — 25-27, 31
    Crabmeat Stuffed — 32, 33
    Sautéed — 31, 32
    Scotch — 32
Tumbler - see Pigeon
Turkey — 4-7
    Aging — 5
    Cleaning — 5
    Roast — 5, 6
    Roast with Sausage & Orange — 6, 7

# Index

| | |
|---|---|
| Turtle | 58-61, 77 |
|     Broiled Steaks | 60, 61 |
|     Cleaning | 58, 59 |
|     Sautéed with Cream Gravy | 60 |
|     Soup | 59, 60 |
| Turtle Dove- see Pigeon | |
| Walleye - see Pickerel | |
| Walleyed Pike - see Pickerel | |
| Warmouth - see Panfish | |
| Whistler - see Duck | |
| Whistler of the Rockies | 74 |
| White Bass - see Bass | |
| White Perch - see Perch | |
| White Pickerel - see Muskellunge | |
| Wichita Spotted Bass - see Bass | |
| Woodchuck | 73 |
| Woodcock | 15, 16 |
|     Aging | 15 |
|     Broiled | 15, 16 |
|     Roast | 15 |
| Wood Duck - see Duck | |
| Yellow Bass - see Bass | |
| Yellow Perch - see Perch | |